Mission My Town

Mission My Town

Finding Your Purpose in the Here and Now

MARK HEIN

Scott,

Thank you for all you do for our town. You are truly living out this book! Let me know if you know of anyone that could benefit from it-

Romans 8:28,

Mark Hein

RESOURCE *Publications* · Eugene, Oregon

MISSION MY TOWN
Finding Your Purpose in the Here and Now

Resource Publications
An Imprint of Wipf and Stock Publishers
199 W. 8th Ave., Suite 3
Eugene, OR 97401

www.wipfandstock.com

PAPERBACK ISBN: 978-1-5326-8358-9
HARDCOVER ISBN: 978-1-5326-8359-6
EBOOK ISBN: 978-1-5326-8360-2

Manufactured in the U.S.A.   04/18/19

Contents

1

Anything

"EVEN IF I HAVE to die with you, I will never disown you!" Peter's eyes narrowed and locked with Jesus' compassionate gaze with an intensity and determination that was sincere and from the very deepest part of his heart. The other weary and emotionally exhausted disciples insisted earnestly the same as Jesus looked each one in the eye. Man after man exclaimed their complete and utter devotion to him. They would do anything for Jesus. Even die.

That is why, moments earlier, his words had hurt them so much. Before Peter and the others pledged their commitment, Jesus had just told them that this very night they would fall away on account of him. They couldn't believe their ears. Their hearts burned with the paradox that they knew what they pledged was true, but Jesus had never, ever told them something that hadn't been true. How could he say that? They had been following him for the last couple of years after giving up their jobs, distancing themselves from family and friends, and putting themselves in harm's way. How could he say this now?

The cool evening breeze whipped their hair and beards as Jesus locked eyes with them now. Only hours ago they had an emotional dinner where Jesus told them something strange about his body and blood being poured out for them. They hadn't understood the symbolism of what Jesus was talking about, but they had walked with their friend and teacher for a couple of years and trusted him. They loved and respected Jesus as much as a human could love and respect another. The grove of olive trees that they now stood under hid part of the moonlight. Jesus looked into their shadowed faces and saw their sincerity and determination. He also saw their future.

You know the rest of the story. Not only did Peter deny him once that night, he denied him three times, even throwing in a swear word for good measure, "****?, I don't know the ***** man!" The other ten had run at the first sign of conflict as well. These men who *loved* and were *committed* to Jesus were not at a place in their faith where they truly would do *anything* for Jesus, as they found out painfully.

I hope you aren't guilty of reading the Bible like I sometimes do: like a history book. Or like a joke that isn't funny anymore because you know the punchline; in this case the stories aren't as powerful to us because we know their endings. The Bible might not be to you (or me at times) what it is intended to be: living and active in our present life.

So, what does this story of these eleven deserters of Jesus have to do with you and with me? How does this story of these guys two thousand years ago intersect my life in this age of internet reliance and sometimes confusing and divisive cultural issues? What does this story mean to me as I read it from my couch? Well, everything.

To fast forward to the end of the disciples' story, they really did mean what they said to Jesus on that fateful night on the Mount of Olives as Roman soldiers were approaching them quietly through the darkened forest, led to Jesus by Judas, his close friend of three years. To fast forward, I will use the words of Mark Batterson, from the awesome book, *All In*:

> In AD 44, King Herod ordered that James the Greater be thrust through with a sword. He was the first of the disciples to be martyred. And so the bloodbath began. Luke was hung by the neck from an olive tree in Greece. Doubting Thomas was pierced with a pine spear, tortured with red-hot plates and burned alive in India. In AD 54, the proconsul of Hierapolis had Phillip tortured and crucified because his wife converted to Christianity while listening to Philip preach. Philip continued to preach while on the cross. Matthew was stabbed in the back in Ethiopia. Bartholomew was flogged to death in Armenia. James the Just was thrown off the southeast pinnacle of the temple in Jerusalem. After surviving the one-hundred foot fall, he was clubbed to death by a mob. Simon the Zealot was crucified by the governor of Syria in AD 74. Judas Thaddeus was beaten to death with sticks in Mesopotamia. Matthias, who replaced Judas Iscariot, was stoned to death and then beheaded. And Peter was crucified upside down at his own request. John the Beloved is the only disciple to die of natural causes,

but that's only because he survived his own execution. When a cauldron of boiling water could not kill John, Emperor Diocletian exiled him to the island of Patmos. He then returned to Ephesus, where he wrote three epistles and died of natural causes about AD 100.[1]

So, evidently, they *were* willing to do as they said, "Even if I (we) must die with you, I (we) will never deny you" (Matt 26:35). So what happened to these eleven men that they would first run like cowards and not evidence their commitment and loyalty to Jesus, and then live and die in a bigger-than-life type of faith? What happened to these men that took them from saying they would do anything for Jesus, then failing to do so, then fully doing *anything and everything* for Jesus, as evidenced by their lives described in Acts and their deaths described above?

My hope is that you saw the title of this book or heard its contents from a friend and were drawn to how your life can best be used to serve Jesus where you are at *right now* and in the place you are at *right now*. You are probably someone who wants to live a life of significance and who wants to better understand how you can use your time, talents, and treasure to really impact the people around you. If so, I am so glad you picked up this book.

However, none of this will happen if you are still in the spiritual place that the disciples first were on the Mount of Olives. Quite possibly you might think you would "do anything" and "die" for Jesus, when in reality you struggle even to *live* for him. This is the struggle common to believers and that is okay. However, to start this book, I am asking you to consider if you would be willing to *do anything* or *give up anything* that Jesus tells you to along the way.

Would you obey if the Holy Spirit moves in your heart to:

Do your job differently?

Take a different job?

Lead your family differently?

Love your roommates, spouse, fiancé, and friends differently?

Enter a new friendship to influence someone for Jesus?

Step back from a relationship you know is toxic and holding you back?

Move?

Stay?

You see, if we are to enter this journey of Mission My Town together, it will be a waste of your time if you aren't in a place to truly do *anything*

1. Batterson, *All In*, 23

for Jesus. You most likely won't be called to die like the disciples. But you could be asked along the way to die to something about or inside yourself, only to gain something far greater. Jesus is sometimes about addition by subtraction. You see, this is the same risk and decision I am making in writing this book. God prompted me to write it and to *live it* along the way. To do so has required me to die to my naturally protective nature and share struggles, victories, sadness, and joy. The writing has required me to die to some of the inner voices in my head that say, "What makes you qualified to lead people on this journey" or "What do you really have to offer?" But I have chosen to die to myself in these areas because I am hopeful that you will die to whatever may be holding you back from being the version of you that God created you fearfully and wonderfully to be. I want to do anything I can do to help others live how God intended for them.

Think about the disciples on the Mount of Olives and subsequent denial of Jesus. Then think about each one in his respective death, knowing he did what was most required of each of us in our earthly time: *they did what they were supposed to do.* They were a few heartbeats away from seeing God and hearing, "Well done, good and faithful servant."

Before we begin this journey together, I want you to be really open to *anything* that God tells you along the way. My greatest prayer, desire, and purpose in taking a risk in writing is so that you may discover how to best *do what you are supposed to do* right now in this stage of your adventure and journey with Jesus.

Take a risk. Join an adventure. Open your heart to the gift that God wants to give you: a life that is more full and meaningful than anything you can dream up on your own. Leave this experience forever changed because of your obedience and open heart.

JOURNAL AND REFLECTION QUESTIONS:

1. Has God already started to speak to you about something he wants you to die to, let go of, restart, or eliminate?

2. What is something that needs to be "different" about the current you or your current life in order for Jesus to use you best?

3. Are you willing to start this journey by looking in the "spiritual mirror" and reflecting upon whether you are willing to do "anything" and "everything" that he might ask you to do in your adventure?

2

What Is Your Africa?

MY WIFE, LORI, HAS always been more spiritual than me, and it probably started way before we met. I grew up pretending that I was the player hitting the game-winning jump shot at the buzzer, or hauling in the long touchdown catch as the final seconds ticked away. While I was busy being the star player of a fictitious team I made up, playing against the likes of Michael Jordan or Larry Bird, Lori pretended she was a missionary. As a young girl, she pretended she was Gladys Aylward impacting China. She pretended she was the female version of Jim Elliot converting the Auca tribe of eastern Ecuador. Lori was Amy Carmichael serving orphans in India. Myself? I didn't even know about these great heroes of the faith. From a young age Lori knew she was called to ministry.

Lori probably always knew she would be a missionary to some people who desperately needed it. Growing up in a more denominational setting, I was a little bit slower to join the missionary party. Hearing about people going to the far reaches of the world excited Lori like very few other things do. I shared this enthusiasm—for them. If I were to be completely honest, words like India, China, Africa sounded like great places to do ministry, but I think I secretly hoped God wouldn't choose me to be the one to go. I am a high school teacher, so I am used to asking questions and then having students avert their gaze, praying that I wouldn't call on them.

There may have been a little bit of that with me and God. Well, maybe a lot bit.

Every close friend that we knew that was going someplace across our great planet gave Lori a tinge of excitement, followed closely and resoundingly by a tinge of disappointment that we weren't the ones going. We have spent years pouring into young people through my job as a teacher and coach (basketball and tennis) and our shared ministry through Young Life, an outreach organization for high school students. We have been blessed to mentor thousands of young friends. We have financially supported their trips to Central America, Africa, China, Dominican Republic, Ireland; the list is long. I had been happy to send and help finance, but more eager to understand how I could best serve God within my borders. Maybe a better way would be to say, within my comfort zone.

Then some of our closest friends actually did make a decision to go to Africa. Like, *for real*. One of my closest friends, Ryan, actually was obedient and answered the call for him, his wife and two daughters to go to one of the poorest countries in the world, Malawi. They risked health scares, loss of income, misunderstanding from family and friends, and much comfort to do what God asked them to do. It was a life changing experience for not only them, but also for those of us close to them who supported them through prayer, financially, etc. We got to see a family that had hardly traveled at all, with no mission background in their extended families, hear and actually obey God and go. It was life-changing to Facetime my friend Ryan and hear only every fourth word, trying to make sense of the conversation, and more importantly, make sense of the difficult life that they had chosen and that God had asked for them. Ryan and Kelli had said "yes" to the command God had given to them. They had come to the point where they were ready to do "anything" that God asked. In my heart, I truly wanted to be in this place of obedience as well.

Fortunately for me, by this time God had been wrestling with me. In Genesis 32, Jacob also wrestled with God. It is a story I am not sure I still understand, but I do know that it left Jacob a changed man. As Jacob traveled away from his father-in-law's home, ready to make a home and a name of his own, God interrupted him. By this time he had two wives and eleven sons. One night he sent this big tribe across the ford of the Jabbok, as well as all of his possessions and then he stayed behind. (My first thought is that eleven kids would maybe cause me to try to find ways to linger behind as well. I can barely manage two kids, but I am not sure that is a biblical interpretation.) That night, as Jacob was alone, he wrestled with "a man" until daybreak. I have so many questions for God about this phrase, but Jacob later says that it was the place that he saw "God face to face." This encounter left Jacob different in two ways. One was physical. God wrenched his hip so much that he limped after this time. Another way Jacob was different was that during this rather bizarre and confusing encounter, God also gave him a new name and a new life purpose. God told him that he would now be called Israel, meaning "he struggles with God."

Have you wrestled with God ever in the dead of the night? Have you wondered if you are on his best path? Have you wondered what he wants and if that is different than what you want for your life? Have you ever wondered if you were even sure that you *wanted* to find out what God wanted? I had wrestled with God in this way. Recently, I came across this portion of a journal entry that I had written and shared with some close friends at the time:

> I have been reading through Chip Ingram's book on Romans 12 called *Living on the Edge*.[1] It has really given me a lot to consider in the few chapters I have read. I wonder if I have truly surrendered my future to Jesus. Chip writes, "We live as though a total commitment to God would be a crushing blow to our personal dreams and future happiness" . . . sometimes I feel like this may be true of me. He also says, "as long as you maintain control of your life, you will be always be destined to get only what you can provide for your life, not what God really wants to give you" and "What would happen in your life if you actually began to believe that God was really FOR you" and "surrender is the only channel through which God's best and biggest blessings flow. He loves you. He is for you. He wants the very, very best for you." These have caused so much introspection. I have long been a Christian and have tried to really teach and coach for Jesus. However, I wonder if I have ever really been open to the possibility of not teaching/coaching.

Through this process God rocked my world. Lori had also recently read *Anything* by Jennie Allen and suggested I read it as well. Just like Jennie and her husband, Zac, we laid awake praying that we would be willing to do "anything" that God asked us to do—that we would be willing to understand how to join Jesus in whatever he asked, whether it be global, local, internal, financial, or so on. It was a desperate and, at the same time, beautiful time to walk through this with my wife.

At some point, it really becomes about who Jesus *is*, just like when he asked the disciples in Mark 8:29, "Who do you same I am?" I wonder if

1. Ingram, *Living On Edge*, 20–35

you have ever really deeply considered your answer to that question. Who does Mark Hein say Jesus is? Who does (your name) say Jesus is? It is a question and an answer that makes all the difference. Is he God or is he also *Lord*? He is either Lord of *all* or not Lord at all. I realized that Jesus had been *mostly* Lord to me. I believed in him, I believed he died on the cross for me, and I trusted him . . . mostly. The problem is Jesus doesn't desire to be mostly Lord. There really isn't such a thing. Revelation 3:15–16: "I know your deeds, that you are neither cold nor hot, I wish that you were either one or the other! So, because you are lukewarm, neither hot nor cold, I am about to spit you out of my mouth." Wow! That is not mincing any words. That is telling it like it is. Jesus is making it clear he wants "all in" Christians. And "all in" means trusting him with our past, present, and future. It means fully trusting in his love and kindness and wisdom that he has the best plan for our life. It might be different than the one that we come up with on our own, but it will be better.

I had struggled with God about the control of my life and was now ready to have my hip wrenched or whatever he wanted to do to me. I was ready to obey. I was ready to do *anything* that God asked us to do. Lori had always been ready to obey. She shared that God had placed a verse on her heart. Not for her. Not for me. But for us together. The verse was Isaiah 26:8: "Yes, Lord, walking in the ways of your laws, we wait for You; Your name and renown are the desires of our hearts." Again, just as God had shared this with her first, the goosebumps on my arm and the stirring in my heart made me deeply know to the bottom of my toes that this verse was for us. We committed to "walking and waiting" and seeking his "renown." It was about then things got confusing for Lori and myself.

Our "Africa" became Austin, Texas.

Some acquaintances of ours committed to starting a church in Austin. I didn't think much about it at the time but stored it in my heart. Lori prayed and thought a ton about it. Slowly, Austin entered more of our conversations. It went from that to being a seemingly constant message. All of a sudden, as I was ordering my grande mocha or iced coffee, every car in front of me seemed to have Texas plates. At every turn we met a stranger, they were from Austin, had a relative in Austin, and so on. Songs came on the radio; the band or producer was from Austin. Authors of books we were reading were from Austin. A young woman who had lived awhile with us decided to go to Austin. The CrossFit fanatics we met were from Austin. I turned on ESPN and Stephen F. Austin was on the TV. We couldn't escape thinking about Austin, as it seemed like God inundated us with images and messages about this great city on the south. So we prayed even more about it and wondered if this was the "anything" that God had been nudging our hearts toward for some time. We decided we needed to really consider it.

So, despite any real tangible job opportunities or even the real financial resources to do it, we decided to be faithful and visit Austin. We loved the city. It was not at all what we thought of when we thought of Texas. It was very much like the tattooed, coffee-soaked city of our home Seattle. It was hip, lively, and growing. It was in a beautiful area with a river running through it, close to the Texas hill country, and to top it off it was the climate that Lori would love: hot and even hotter. We absolutely loved it and knew that we were to be faithful to consider it. We even had BBQ (of course) with the church planters from our area—we loved their vision and knew we could be on the same page to join God in what he was doing in Austin through this church. I am a bit of a real estate nerd, so I could tell you what areas of Austin we would want to be in, but more reasonably, what areas we could afford. We put Austin, our "Africa," at Jesus' feet and waited.

And waited.

And then, very confusingly, our "Africa" wasn't Austin after all.

We weren't supposed to go.

We didn't know why.

And this wrecked our world for a while.

We never *knew* we were going to Austin, but inside it felt like it probably might happen. But a funny thing happened. The job possibilities that seemed to be coming open didn't come open after all. We had been so open-minded and open-handed to the idea of this move that frankly it was a disappointment that God wasn't calling us there. We had handed Austin to God and he had handed it back. Honestly, with sadness, we recognized that we were being asked to stay. In our limited understanding, we felt like we were a well-read book that was being put back on the shelf. We suddenly wondered why God would de-purpose our lives. The adrenaline and excitement were followed by tears, disappointment, and wondering why he had let us get excited. How were we ever going to get excited about this place in which we had already lived for over ten years?

I wonder if you also have ever stepped out in faith to really consider what he wanted from you and been "let down" by his answer or, worse yet, his seeming lack of an answer. Here we were, ready to *go anywhere* and then seemed to have a *somewhere*, and then realized we were right back where we started.

But maybe, just maybe, where we started was and is where we were most meant to be in this season of our lives.

Maybe our "Africa" was Lake Stevens.

Maybe our mission field was right in the place where God had kept us.

We were ready to go anywhere, but he seemed to desire us right here.

At the beginning of our journey, I asked you to be open to anything that God asked you to do. He might have been asking you to move the past year and you have been reluctant to do so. He may have been asking you to downsize from that 4,500 square foot house into something more modest to better serve financial needs around you. He might have been telling you to find a new job in which he could use your skillset better. If he has been asking you to go to a cross-cultural mission field, move houses, change jobs, etc., I ask you to be obedient and *do it*.

And if he has you *here*, where you are right now, let's explore how he wants you to make it your Mission My Town. How can you take your heart to serve God in the most impactful way possible and pour it out into the place you currently live? How can your mission to Africa or your mission to China become your Mission My Town?

Mission My Town is simply looking at where you are as God's greatest mission call on your life. My goal is to encourage you to open your eyes to God's purpose for you in the here and now. It might mean flipping your whole perspective that you need to travel elsewhere to truly be your most impactful self for the kingdom of God. It might require you to rethink your relationships, activities, and basic life functions in your town to heed his final command to "go make disciples." I am excited to enter into this adventure with you and I am asking God to reveal his best intent for your life, right where you are.

JOURNAL AND REFLECTION QUESTIONS:

1. Have you ever experienced God calling you toward something or someplace and felt your feet pulled out from under you?

2. Have you ever felt de-purposed in a ministry, calling, relationship, etc. that you knew he had been previously calling you toward?

3. Do you feel like you have ever looked at your town as your biggest mission field?

3

Discontent

MY WIFE, LORI, AND I live an amazing, blessed life. We of course have had the bumps and bruises of life: deaths of loved ones, confusing turns or endings to dreams, times of sickness, and struggles with finances, relationships, or our own inner selves. However, we have good jobs that bring meaning to ourselves and to others. We are professionals who view our jobs as callings and not simply something that pays the bills. We have two beautiful, vibrant kids that are just beginning middle school. Our kids go to great public schools and have (for the most part) loved their teachers. We own (or at least are paying on) a middle-income house on a cul-de-sac in a very family-oriented community. We have had parents that have loved us well and stayed together for many years. We have awesome friends that would do anything to help us at the drop of a hat. We know the friends we "do life with" have our backs and love us. Our marriage is healthy. We feel blessed beyond belief that we have been able to spend our days with our best friend for the past twenty years. And we love Jesus full on.

So, why in the world would the twins of unrest and discontent follow us both as we look at the dent we are making on the world?

It goes beyond the normal wistfulness that a middle-aged dad gets as he pulls up to the stoplight in his used, dented, well-traveled mini-van (the throne of most every family man) and sees the younger version of himself in the car next to him. For me, it is not so much the guy in the sports car with the well-manicured blonde next to him the front seat. For me, this comes when I see the adventurous guy in the four-door Jeep with the residue of mud on the windows and body from some fun he just had. Everyone probably has that slightly wistful feeling when seeing their younger self and remembering the big vision of the super-sized splash he or she was planning on making upon the world.

My big splash was to be a division-one head college basketball coach and to use this position and perch to impact the world for Jesus. For Lori, this was to be in public office and be one of the most well-respected business women in politics to impact the world. We have both come to joyfully understand and embrace the different plan that God set before us and we have been blessed enough to travel. In actuality, he created a life for us better and more meaningful and rich than we could have ever have come up with on our own. This discontent was not the sadness of dreams that had not materialized.

This was different. This came back to some questions that you might have also:

Am I making a difference?

Does what I do daily really impact the world and, even more, God's kingdom?

Is this really the life that God wants me to live?

Would I be better able to serve God in a different corner of the world?

Am I God's best version of myself? Am I using my gifts in the manner that he intends?

Am I in the most effective place, job, and relationships that God can use to impact the world?

If any of these are questions you are asking, have asked, or might now be nudged to ask, then I am very excited to share this adventure with you. In the next few chapters I pray that you will join me in the journey to explore these questions. I am about truth and transparency, so I want to get this one thing straight: I am not an expert as I explore this with you. I am traveling these questions with you. If you were hoping to pick up this book and explore the inner workings of a great expert, I will tell you that is not my perspective. I write these words not as having fully attained the answers, but as one that would like to come closer to being able to more confidently answer them. I write as God prompts me to ask these for myself and invite you in on the journey to see what he would tell each of us. No doubt the answers will be different for you than me or somebody else. But I believe the asking and answering of these questions makes all the difference in our lives. This brings me to a moment that happened a couple of year ago.

We had settled into comfortable couches, loveseats, and a couple wooden chairs from the kitchen. Some people sipped coffee, others ate warm dessert as we gathered in the living room of a large, inviting home with an open layout. Kids' voices could be heard faintly outside as our never-quiet kids explored the open space of this country home. We could hear some laughing as they bounced on a trampoline. We could hear some younger kids excitedly looking at chickens and playing with a puppy. It was a clear, late August night following a sunny day. But these details weren't the most important details. I found those as I looked around at the group assembled.

Lori and I, in conjunction with our good friends, Kyle and Heather, had invited some people we felt might be in the same spiritual "place." There were couples that had been married for more than fifteen years. There were some single Young Life leaders in the group. There was an NBA basketball player and his girlfriend. She just came along because she happened to be at his house, and "it sounded strangely interesting." There was a high school guy who was surprisingly comfortable in this setting with adults. There was a family bravely considering God's next step for their careers. The room was a cross-section of our community, and they were all experiencing holy discontent.

This was a phrase I borrowed from Lori to initiate the meeting. To be fair, she had also borrowed it from a Barna research project.[1] The phrase was used in the progression of faith in following Jesus. The study described ten steps of spiritual maturity including the following: being ignorant of sin, aware of sin, knowing that sin might impact your life, seeking forgiveness and choosing Jesus as Savior, then step 5 which is religious activity. Most American Christians stop at step 5, "Religious Activity." This was the jump from accepting what Jesus did for us and making him Lord, then proceeding to live a spiritual life of church, Bible studies, maybe a small group or a Saturday morning fellowship group, doing things that help draw us closer to Jesus.

Very few people get past step 5, and often Christians only get to step 6 after fifteen to thirty years at step 5. Step 6 is "holy discontent." This is where people start asking "Is this all?" or "Have I become the person God made me to be?" The Holy Spirit really begins to stretch their perspective

1. Barna Group, "Research," paragraph 10.

on their life. The final stages of spiritual maturity from Barna are being broken and becoming dependent on God, surrendering and submitting to God, experiencing peace with God, and finally fully and totally being able to love others.

In this moment in this room, it seemed that most of us were at this place of "holy discontent." A trickle of sweat made its way down my forehead as I uncomfortably took the leap to talk about my journey to this conversation, as well as the path Lori and I had traveled together the past couple months. Before long, the Holy Spirit took over; I lost myself in trying to explain the holy discontent that I felt and thought others might also share.

I did my best to explain how my study of Romans 12 had really caused me to look at whether I had surrendered everything. I referenced something I had recently learned from the Kyle Idleman, who describes that when the Knights of Templar were baptized they completely immersed themselves into the water. Well, not really. They held their swords above their heads and out of the water as a sign that everything except the swords was holy.[2] Everything was to be done for the Lord, but the sword had its own purpose. I shared how that example resonated with me. Was my job, my career, my professional aspirations, or hopes my "sword" that I held out of the baptism water? Was I shortchanging Jesus? I shared that I was now at the "anything" phase for Jesus. I was ready to hear about what was next. Lori was also. I spoke of our incredible small group that cared for each other and met each other's needs. It is a very special group that I likened to having a "spider web" of care and concern for one another. They would (and had) drop everything to help other people in need in our group, but I still felt like it wasn't a ripple effect that was aimed to bring about change in our community. This was a holy discontent in my life. Jesus told us to take care of the widows and orphans. Jesus told us to feed the hungry. Jesus told us to go make disciples of all nations. My discontent was that I was doing not many of these things and didn't see too many people with a passion to do so either.

I spoke of the day that Lori came home and announced that God had told her we should take a mission trip. I remembered the extreme uneasiness I felt, as I was sure that meant finding a plane ticket to some corner of the world I wasn't sure I wanted to go to. We had already talked about how I felt called to being where we were at least one more year. But as she

2. Forrest, "I'll Have Jesus," lines 1–10.

announced, "I think we are to take a mission trip to our community." I was covered in goosebumps as the Holy Spirit confirmed this in my inmost being as only he can. We excitedly talked about what this meant for us. We began to pray. We began to really hold on to Isaiah 26:8, "Yes, LORD, walking in the way of your laws, we wait for you; your name and renown are the desire of our hearts."

I was so excited to change as I realized this verse honestly had previously been more like Mark Hein 1:1, "Maybe, Lord. Sometimes walking in the way of your laws, sometimes walking in just what I want to do, I wait for you to give me what I want. My fame and my comfort are the desire of my heart."

Both Lori and I shared. Our basic message was: "Do you have any similar holy discontent? We are ready to do whatever God wants us to do. We are in a phase of waiting for him, but also actively looking for ways to join him in what he is doing around us in Lake Stevens. We completely desire to impact this community for Jesus in his best way. We don't know what it looks like, or even how it relates to you all. It sounds crazy, but what do you think?"

I had begun this night by playing the song "God of this City" by Chris Tomlin. The words had become a mantra of sorts in my heart for the previous few weeks. It had been a hymn sung at a marriage retreat Lori and I had been able to attend. This had been a moment that drew tears of confirmation out of my beautiful and tender wife as to it pertaining to our town. It had been a moment that brought on Holy Spirit goosebumps from my head to toe as I fully realized God was the God of Lake Stevens. The words of this hymn now formed the backdrop for what people soon began to share this night as we gathered at Kyle and Heather's beautiful home.

Slowly at first, but picking up steam, words began to stream from one person, then the next. People spoke with similar hearts of loving Jesus like crazy, being challenged to "go bigger" but wondering what that meant. Every single person in the room spoke about this holy discontent in a very personal way that was a slightly different version of the previous person. Some stories brought tears, some brought smiles, all brought Jesus to the forefront.

It was an incredibly comforting feeling to be in the midst of people who: wanted more; wanted to love people more like Jesus loves; wanted to impact those "unreachable" in the community, or at least the "unreached"; wanted to impact young and old; wanted a non-church feel to something where anyone felt welcome; wanted authentic community; wanted to put down all facades and masks and have a genuine place where all were welcome. The wants that people shared were varied, but had the underlying holy discontent for our town.

The evening ended with a challenge for us to really pray about what this all meant and reconvene in a week. We challenged each other to really dwell in prayer on what God might be doing here. As we lingered in good conversations, with kids now filling the room and bringing chatter, the joy was obvious, even if the mission of the group was not yet clear.

The one thing that was clear: we were all called to go on a mission in our very own backyard and community. We were ready for Mission My Town.

JOURNAL AND REFLECTION QUESTIONS:

1. Think about Barna's ten steps of spiritual maturity. Be honest with yourself and assess which step you think you are on today.

2. Look at the questions below from early in the chapter and pick one or two to reflect on:

   Am I making a difference?

   Does what I do daily really impact the world and, even more, God's kingdom?

   Is this really the life that God wants me to live?

   Would I be better able to serve God in a different corner of the world?

   Am I God's best version of myself? Am I using my gifts in the manner that he intends?

   Am I in the most effective place, job, and relationships that God can use to impact the world?

4

The Great Omission

IMAGINE BEING JESUS ON one of the last occasions that he gets to talk to his disciples. What a crazy three years he has had with these eleven very mortal guys that are gathered before him on a mountain in Galilee in Matthew 28. I wonder how many thoughts were racing through his mind as he looked back on their intent gazes. There is hardly a sound other than the wind whipping their long hair as they stand atop the mountain from which Jesus will deliver one of his final messages to them.

Their tired, gaunt faces look at their friend and master. There is a palpable tentativeness about them as they think through how they left Jesus on his own to face soldiers, a court of law, and the penalty of death. They have a laundry list of ways they have denied him and let him down in the very recent past. Conversations, arguments, questions, and sermons from their journey with him flood their minds as they see their friend who has risen from the dead and is now before them. They remember arguing about such trivial things like which one of them was the greatest. They reflect on requests to sit at Jesus' side in heaven. They think about the many times Jesus sighed and slowly explained another parable that they hadn't understood. Here they were facing a friend whom they had let down, who had died a gruesome death, rose from the dead, and now stood before them. Now, here he was to give them some final words. This would be goodbye.

What would you have told them? What choice words would you have passed on to the people who would lead your mission forward? What words would you have chosen that could change these people and the direction of all history? How would you frame what faith, ministry, and life should look like

The words that Jesus decides to share are beautiful, poignant, instructive, and encouraging. Rather than words of condemnation or setting the bar low, Jesus gives them a purpose and support for it. "Go and make disciples of all nations, baptizing them in the name of the Father and of the Son and of the Holy spirit, and teaching them to obey everything I have commanded you. And surely I am with you always, to the very end of the age" (Matt 28:19–20).

To work through these words of Jesus, I am tremendously comforted to know that the Jesus I love and desire to serve leaves us with this last sentence. His parting thought is that he wants you and I to know, above all else, he is *with* us. Not only is he *for* us, not only does he *love* us, not only does he *care* for us, but he is *with* us. What a deep, comforting thought. This world brings so many tough things. Being a follower of Jesus does not promise a carefree life. In fact, Jesus promises us we will have persecutions in this world. However, we love an all-powerful God who is not only capable of changing history, he is also capable of dwelling with us as we navigate our lives.

Jesus' words in Matthew 28 are often called "the great commission." He is calling this ramshackle, mistake-ridden group of people to a great task. He is also calling or "commissioning" you and me to this same task. Do you see what I see, when you look at the disciples? They desired to follow Jesus and obey him. They told him this expressly. They had given the last three years of their lives to serve him. They had made a costly decision to follow him, giving up their jobs and time with people they loved to join him on his mission on earth. But they also showed pride, lack of faith at times, jealousy, and even went back on their word in the heat of the moment. If you are honest with yourself, can you point to times in your life with these same failings? I know I can—and I don't even have to look too far in the rear view mirror to do so.

But Jesus called them, this group of imperfect people, to a wonderful mission way bigger than their skillset, experience, or comfort level. He is calling you and me to the same mission, the great mission. This mission is to make disciples of people. It is to join Jesus in the process of people meeting him, giving their lives to him, and becoming disciples. Not only converts, but disciples. We are called to come alongside people, love them, show them Jesus, and help them grow in their faith.

Have you ever experienced the following scenario in a church? The pastor or speaker finishes the message, the lights dim, the guitar music cues up, and you are asked to close your eyes. The pastor then talks to people that might be making a decision to accept grace and Jesus and give their lives to him. "With heads bowed and eyes closed for privacy, please raise your hand if you made this decision today. On my left, to your right, raise your eyes and hand and let our eyes meet." He then scans the rooms and says "amen" when he sees a convert. He ends with, "The Bible says that when this happens there is a party in heaven, let's clap and join this party that is happening in heaven right now for these six people who have expressed a desire to follow Jesus." I have experienced this countless times and I love it, but sometimes it leaves me asking questions. The next week the pastor might talk about how many people gave their lives to Jesus last week and how amazing that was. And that is amazing. It is life changing. But there is more to our great mission. We are called to make *disciples*, not only converts. I love conversion. I also think it is equally important to be intentional about how we are going to help these people learn how to study God's Word, learn how to follow Jesus on a daily basis, and learn how to be a disciple. Later in our time together, we will talk more about what it means to "make disciples" of those we are called to love and serve.

Making disciples was important to Jesus. I picture the scene described in Matthew 13 and see Jesus kind of like a rock star. He sat down to teach and people just showed up. Lots of people. And more people. So many people, he got into a boat, pushed out a bit, and began to teach. I love visualizing this scene of Jesus patiently and expertly teaching from a wooden boat to people crammed into every inch of the shore. I will use the words directly from Jesus in verses 3–9:

> Then he told them many things in parables, saying: "A farmer went out to sow his seed. As he was scattering the seed, some fell along the path, and the birds came and ate it up. Some fell on rocky places, where it did not have much soil. It sprang up quickly, because the soil was shallow. But when the sun came up, the plants were scorched, and they withered because they had no root. Other seed fell among thorns, which grew up and choked the plants. Still other seed fell on good soil, where it produced a crop—a hundred, sixty or thirty times what was sown. Whoever has ears, let them hear. (Matt 13:3–9)

There are four types of soil that Jesus describes. The final three examples all involve "conversion." In two cases, the plants that Jesus is describing represent faith that grows up, then is choked by rocky soil or thorns. Jesus himself says:

> The seed falling on rocky ground refers to someone who hears the word and at once receives it with joy. But since they have no root, they last only a short time. When trouble or persecution comes because of the word, they quickly fall away. The seed falling among the thorns refers to someone who hears the word, but the worries of this life and the deceitfulness of wealth choke the word, making it unfruitful. But the seed falling on good soil refers to someone who hears the word and understands it. This is the one who produces a crop, yielding a hundred, sixty or thirty times what was sown. (Matt 13:20–23)

The last one is what we want to help people toward. We want to make fruitful disciples.

As we continue to work through the great commission, at the very beginning Jesus tells his followers (then and also now) to "go and make disciples of all nations." Does this phrase scare you or excite you?

Picture yourself as a "missionary"; seriously, do it. Really, I know the drill. I have read countless books that have asked me to take a pause and do something and I am oh-so-guilty of not doing. What do you think of when you see yourself as a "missionary?"

Are you mentally picturing yourself dressed differently and learning the customs and culture of a country much different than your own? Are you envisioning yourself learning a new language to better connect with the people around you? Do you see yourself speaking in front of a big crowd in a poorly lit building in a developing nation? Do you see yourself drilling for clean drinking water in an area that people are literally dying because they can't drink clean water? Do you see yourself in Africa surrounded by orphans, teaching them English? Do you see yourself on a team in the Dominican Republic, building a small home for people who are living in a cardboard substitute for a home, the home that you and I take for granted? Do you picture yourself on a plane, flying to a different corner of the world to do the work God is placing inside of you?

This may be where God is calling you. And if so, I am elated for you. I seriously am. God has called us to go into *all the world*. If God has been tugging on your heart, giving you internal and external reminders constantly, then be obedient. Go. Go where he calls. Join his mission where he has been calling you to join him in efforts to save the lost and broken in that corner of the world.

However, I am confident that many of you just don't see yourself in this place in your life. Maybe you just graduated college and have the mountain of student debt that so many of us have experienced. Possibly, you are retired and aren't in a physical, financial, or emotional place to uproot your life. Quite certainly, there are many reading this book who love Jesus, but are just trying to get the kids to the right soccer practice and pay the utility and Netflix bills. Maybe you are engaged fully in a job that you couldn't leave right now. Maybe you are caring for a parent or someone stricken with cancer and couldn't abandon at this juncture of your life. Maybe you are like many that only get partial custody of your amazing children and have rearranged your whole personal and work life to be closer to your kids.

Whether you are in a phase of life that you can't go elsewhere or whether you simply don't feel called, you are a missionary. If you love Jesus, his great commission is to you too. And I am excited to share what God has been placing on my heart to join him in his mission around me.

"Go and make disciples of all nations": the Great Commission.

Unfortunately, our American Christian culture has also been responsible for what I call the *great omission* regarding the same command.

For too long, the words "all nations" have not really meant that to our American Christian culture. Your nation is part of all nations. We are not only called to be sent out globally, but also into the world right outside and inside our own front door. Jesus called us to the same great mission whether it is in China or Chicago. Whether it is in India or Indiana. Whether it is in Mexico or Montreal. Whether it is in Laos or Lake Stevens. You are called to mission where you are right now.

Think about the people who have most impacted your faith. Seriously, think about the people that have really caused you to first see Jesus or experience him more fully. It may well be Billy Graham, Chip Ingram, Rick Warren, Beth Moore, or Kay Arthur. But more likely, it is someone you really know—someone who has lived out their faith and took time to share that faith and life with you. Personal discipleship with someone they love and respect often has a bigger impact in people's lives than words from a famous and gifted speaker. That is the real crux and heart of our Mission My Town. We want to be intentional and purposeful about our life so that we don't miss the chance to have this impact on others. I have been so impacted by ministries like Young Life, which uses the phrase, "Earn the right to be heard." Through relationship and living our lives, we have the opportunity to tremendously influence those we know and love.

So, back to the question, "Are you a missionary?" If you desire to follow Jesus and the thing he most wants you to accomplish with your life is to make disciples, then you have been called to Mission Your Town. It is not some special thing for the spiritual giants of the world. If we are following Christ, we are called to mission.

JOURNAL AND REFLECTION QUESTIONS:

1. What do you think of when you see yourself as a "missionary"?

2. Is God calling you right now to a mission outside of our borders? If so, reflect on that. Be obedient to what he tells you in prayer.

3. Who are the most influential people in your own life spiritually?

4. What is your reaction so far to what you have been reading in *Mission My Town*?

5

Circles of Intention

MY FRIENDS THINK I am over the top in my desire to go and be deep. I won't lie; they are probably completely correct. In terms of conversations, I heard myself once say to someone, "Life is too short for small talk." It surprised me when I said it as I had never really thought about it before the words leaked out of my mouth. However, as I experience life and relationships, it certainly is true. I value people who can go deep and I sometimes can be dismissive of those who seemingly don't want to, or for whatever reason cannot. Conversations that get beyond the weather or Seahawks game are always a bonus. It can sometimes be awkward for others how quickly I go for depth.

On my work desk I have a sign that Lori gave me that reads, "Live with Intention." I do want to try to live *for* purpose and *with* purpose. Every year I ask God to give me a verse of the year and a theme of the year. My buddies who know me very well always know what my focus is and help keep me accountable to this theme as the busyness of life invariably takes my focus away. My friends Jeff and Ryan have joined me for years in asking me periodically about it and then truly listening and supporting me in the quest that God has given me for that year.

Sometimes these themes have been complex with words for every major area of my life; sometimes, like this year, it is a single word. This particular year the word God gave me is "grace"—for myself, for others. And certainly to understand the grace he shows me. As a teacher and coach and someone who ministers to students, our "year" is the school year. Every

August, I make time to get away for a couple of hours at a time for several days spread out over the month. Specifically, I ask God to give me a verse in which he would like me to dwell deeply. I journal, spend time in the Word, and then spend time listening, trying to drown out the squeaky hamster wheel that is my brain. I am not always good at slowing my mind or life down to hear God's answers. However, in this area of my life I have been able to do so, and God has never failed to nudge my heart in a particular direction with a particular verse.

One wonderful opportunity I had this past year was to see my wife in her element. Lori is a speaker and a coach. She coaches business professionals and people in ministry. I know I am partial, but she is a tremendous speaker. She blends humor, depth, and an awareness of her audience that makes her a fantastic speaker. This particular time she had been asked to speak at a staff and spouse retreat for a ministry organization. It doubled as a great getaway for us as a couple. The conference was at the Double T River Ranch in Montana, a classic ranch along the river in the Big Sky beautifulness that is Western Montana. You seriously should Google it and look at the barn. Lori was speaking in the loft of this barn, surrounded by people who were looking to serve Jesus through this ministry. The loft of the barn is beautifully refurbished with wood that has hues of grey and blue with a classic lofted ceiling. It looks out over the beautiful grounds which include a bocce ball court, sand volleyball court, putting green, a small peaceful pond, and above all else, a great view of the river and low-lying mountains. As I looked out the back patio over the view and listened to my wife use her gifts beautifully and effectively for God's kingdom, she said something that stopped me in my tracks and made the spiritual hair stand up on the back of my neck.

"How you spend your days is how you spend your life."

Lori probably borrowed the phrase and you may have heard it before, but I had not. It deeply resonated with me as I was looking for huge purpose and wondering if God was even using my little life that I was trying to give him. This statement is so obvious, but deep in its simplicity. If we are following Jesus well, we are asking the big questions. We are asking if we are on the right and best path to be used in this short life. Like you, I want to have a life that is big for God and full of his story and glory. I look for the big thing: the move to Austin, the call to a different corner of the country or world, a call to a new profession. But sometimes, he calls us right to exactly where we are and to live our daily life with the realization that it is part of the sum of our whole opportunity to glorify his story. Our days, even shrouded in the necessary boredom of paying bills, grocery shopping, studying for finals, driving kids to and fro, making dinner, cleaning toilets, and so on, are all important to the bigger story of our gift to the world and back to God.

Therefore, I am not ashamed to live with intention, and I challenge you to do the same, in a world where depth is a very distant second to the good soundbite, YouTube cat videos, the latest iPhone, The Housewives of _____, and other reality TV that really doesn't often have much to do with reality. So, while you may not be called to what you view as a big mission elsewhere, you are called to a huge mission in the front yard of your life. Be intentional about starting this Mission My Town *today*.

One challenge of this mission for us was to clearly *hear* and *define* the specifics about what God was calling us to in our town. Both Lori and I knew fully that God was calling us to care for, minister to, and love deeply this community we call home. However, in the infancy of this mission, we had struggled to put our finger on exactly what it was and who it was for. We both began to think about our spheres of influence, our current commitments and involvements, as well as our past relationships. Some clarity was given one day when Lori was talking to her best friend, Janet, about some struggles to define her ministry. Janet and her husband, Brian, are close friends of ours and we have seen them grow exponentially in their desire and activity to mission to those around them. They have taken short term mission trips to Asia and also thrown themselves into the ministry field immediately around them. On this day Janet was working through really clarifying her mission.

Lori had Janet draw some circles on a paper. Each circle represented different activities, commitments, groups, ministries, or friend groups that were part of this woman's life. Lori then had her write various peoples' names within these circles to represent those to whom she had connection. As Lori reflected on this later, she shared that it was actually eye-opening to her and she had immediately had the phrase "Circles of Intention" in her head. It is a wonderful phrase that has begun to define our ministry to our town. It is through the natural relationships we have that God desires to use us even deeper. I believe that God wants us to be very intentional in recognizing who these people are, praying for them consistently, and being very intentional about how to either reach these groups to help them become disciples or to take disciples and help them grow deeper roots.

Possibly one of the most valuable experiences we will do together through this book is for you to really clarify your Circles of Intention. Do you remember that college philosophy class most of us hated and few of us passed—the one with Venn diagrams (see below) and truth tables? Think Venn diagrams as you draw these circles of intention. All of your circles might be separate and completely independent from each other, or they might overlap like the Venn diagram. You might journal about it or scribble these circles elsewhere, but for the effectiveness of our journey together, this is something that I really need you to stop reading and go do. So, think long and deeply about all the circles of people you interact with in your life.

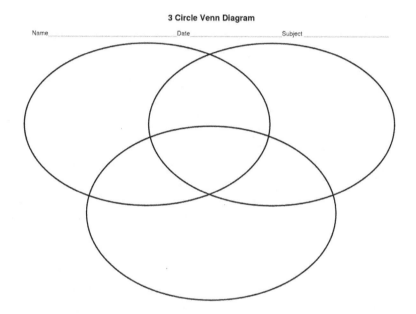

3 Circle Venn Diagram

Name_____ Date_____ Subject_____

6

Light

PICTURE THE BEST VANTAGE point to see your city, town, or region. Envision the best spot to see this place you desire to impact. Picture yourself at this precise location, overlooking this place you now call home.

We live in Lake Stevens in Washington, in the amazingly beautiful, and equally amazingly wet, Pacific Northwest. Our lake is the hub of our town and is frequented by early morning fishermen and water skiers, in addition to wakeboarders, wake surfers, kids and families hanging out at the public beaches later in the day. We even have a community celebration called Aquafest, which is full of activities centered around the lake. It is a beautiful place to live.

For one glorious year, we had the opportunity to live on the lake. It had been a dream of mine to own waterfront property, so this was a special experience. To make a very long story very short, we were doing ministry through Young Life, an outreach to high school kids. A local supporter of Young Life offered us the chance to rent his house on the lake. As only God can arrange, we also had a single mom who was navigating a divorce and she ended up renting our house as we rented the lake house.

This lake house was straight out of the 1970s with wood paneling, outdated fixtures, and the craziest color combinations one could envision. (As a pure random side note: it also had the weirdest, creepiest panic room in the basement with a single phone and nothing else but a lockable door. But I digress.) Two important facts to know about me: I love basketball and anything on the water. This house was the perfect merger of both with its indoor basketball court. It was an amazing house to do ministry for that year and we are forever grateful.

The lake house also had a two-million-dollar view. From the house, one could look down to the one hundred plus feet of lakefront and to the dock. The beach was down a fairly steep hill, so the house set up a good seventy or eighty feet above the level of the lake. It had a tremendous deck that wrapped around the whole lake side of the house and offered amazing views and space to entertain. From this deck, one could see virtually the entire lake. The Fourth of July was fabulous for having people over and watching the fireworks. Fireworks are legal here and the residents do it up like the Boston Tea Party. It is crazy cool on a summer night, tucked in a blanket with family and close friends watching this spectacle.

It is from this deck that I picture Lake Stevens when I pose the task I gave you at the beginning of this chapter. From an Adirondack chair, not only can one see most of the lake, but it offers a spectacular view beyond. In fact, I even had the chance to officiate a wedding at this house for a former student athlete who Lori had discipled as well. The wedding was on the grassy lawn and overlooked this same view I describe. Mount Pilchuck rises out of the distance, and beyond that are the snow-filled Cascade mountains. Bald eagles often fly overhead. This is the view of my town that I cherish.

Let's go back to your viewpoint. Picture yourself there. Picture yourself looking out over your community with a heart to serve this place and impact it for Jesus. Picture this town and feel your desire to join God in his work here as he is the "God of this city." Now, do something different. Visualize yourself at this same vantage point, looking out over your town, but now visualize it being night. There is no moon, but the city or community is lit up by the street lights and house lights. Now, visualize the power going out. You can still make out the skyline, the defining characteristics of this place you call home, but it is dim and difficult to see with much clarity.

In the middle of this scene, picture a light. Picture this light that shines in stark contrast to the murky darkness around it. See the way it illuminates things close by and brings them into the light. Picture the vast difference that this single light has from the rest of the unlit, dark vision of your community.

I, like you, want to be such a light. I want to find the purpose in my community that joins God in his work. I want not only to be this light, but to join other lights to brighten this community for God's glory.

Jesus himself used this same analogy of spiritual impact being light. In Matthew's account of the Sermon on the Mount, Jesus said the following in 5:14–16:

> "You are the light of the world. A city set on a hill cannot be hidden. Nor do people light a lamp and put it under a basket, but on stand, and it gives light to all in the house. In the same way, let your light so shine before others, so that they may see your good works and give glory to your Father who is in heaven."

Our desire is to be such a light. We want the way we lead our families, work our jobs, interact with our professors, conduct our business, the way we recreate, the relationships we foster and invest in, the way we love our spouse, kids, neighbors, and enemies, to be a *light* to our town. Jesus tells us that by so doing, we will not be bringing glory to ourselves, but to him. He gives us a great challenge and goal.

He also gives a qualifier.

Our light is not to be hidden.

It is fascinating to learn about the history and culture that impacted Jesus' teachings. We lose some of his subtle messages by not having a clear picture of the culture and geography of his day. I recently learned that during his Sermon on the Mount, Jesus was teaching somewhere near the sea of Galilee. From where Jesus was, it was less than one hundred miles to the south where the Jordan River flows into the Salt Sea or Dead Sea. Present-day Jordan, Israel, and Palestine border this salty lake. Its surface and shores are about 1,400 feet below sea level, the lowest elevation on Earth's land. It is also over 300 feet deep and is the deepest hypersaline lake in the world. If you have ever accidentally swallowed a mouthful of the Pacific Ocean, you know saltiness. However, to put it into perspective, the Dead Sea is almost ten times as salty as the ocean. In fact, it is so salty that animals and plants cannot survive there, hence its ominous name. It is so salty that people can easily float on its surface. People of his day were familiar with the "salt" of the earth.

However, what is fascinating to me is that while Jesus spoke the Sermon the Mount, there was a community of people living on the western side of the lake known as the Dead Sea Community. These are the people whose scrolls made international news when they were discovered and excavated in the 1950s. These scrolls included some of the oldest known surviving manuscripts that include the Hebrew Bible canon. The people living in this community in the day of Jesus were most likely a monastic community of

Essenes (sect of Jewish people). They had withdrawn from the wickedness of the world and ironically called themselves the "sons of light."

I wonder if Jesus motioned with his head towards the south where these Essenes lived as he said the words in the Sermon on the Mount. I wonder if the people listening realized how significantly different Jesus' words were than the lifestyle of these who had chosen to hide from the world and had turned inward in seeking holiness.

> "You are the light of the world. A city set on a hill cannot be hid. Nor do people light a lamp and put it under a basket, but on a stand, and it gives light to all in the house. In the same way, let your light shine before others, so that they may see your good works and give glory to your Father who is in heaven" (Matt 5:14–16).

This is the call for us in our communities.

Put your name in the blanks:

"You, _____, are the light of the world (and specifically to your community). _____, let your light shine before (the people in your town), that they may see *your* good works and give glory to your Father who is in heaven."

Let us look to let God use our relationships, jobs, personalities, character, hobbies, influence, and even our enemies, shortcomings, failures, and disappointments to be people who don't hide our faith. Let us not be like the Essenes and think that by hiding our faith or disconnecting from the world we are helping God's cause. Jesus makes it very clear to the contrary.

JOURNAL AND REFLECTION QUESTIONS:

1. What is the vantage point of your town that you pictured at the beginning of the chapter?

2. When we talk about the "light" of your town, who jumps out as a person or family who is a spiritual "difference maker" in your town?

3. What are the areas of your life in your town where you think you are the most light for Jesus?

   In what areas do you feel like God wants you to be more a light for him in your town?

7

Inflow and Outflow

BY NOW, YOU ARE well aware that we live in a community called Lake Stevens. Otherwise, I am a very poor communicator. The actual lake is the center of our community. I mentioned our small-town American event called Aquafest. Aquafest is a step back in time: food booths; carnival rides; cotton candy; elephant ears; corn dogs; pet shows; Miss Aquafest pageant; kiddie rides. Picture a 1954 movie scene and you got it—I feel like Cary Grant is going to walk right down the street as Norman Rockwell paints the event.

I will give you a few trivia facts about the lake itself. It is the largest and deepest lake in Snohomish county. The surface of the lake covers approximately 1,040 square acres. The average depth is 64 feet and the deepest the lake gets is 154 feet. Overall it is said to have good water quality. By now, you are thinking I am channeling my inner "Bill Nye the Science Guy," but I promise I will make a point soon. The lake is fed by three creeks: Lundeen, Stitch, and Kokanee. It then flows out from one primary outflow, the Catherine Creek, which goes to the Little Pilchuck Creek, which eventually pours into the Pilchuck river. Below is a picture of this centerpiece of our town:

So, what is the point of all this information. Fair question. For a few moments I am asking you to consider looking at this lake as a word picture for your soul. I am asking you to make the connection between this body of water and the place in you where God meets you and spiritual things happen. In short, this lake represents your walk with Jesus. In order for things to grow in Lake Stevens and for healthy water to be present, there must be inflow and outflow. Likewise, the way that God designed our spiritual lives to flourish and produce health is that we have the inflow of his power and the Holy Spirit's presence in our lives, as well as the outflow of his love toward others.

A few short years ago, as I mentioned earlier, Lori and I thought we were being called to Austin. We felt so strongly about this possible call that we bought airline tickets, set up meetings, and got ready to travel to Austin to meet with people and hear God. Meanwhile, we had heard that Austin held some really cool things that we didn't want to miss as we traveled there. In addition to listening to God, we wanted to make the trip to explore and experience Austin. We had heard about the wonderful Texas Hill Country west of Austin. We decided we would take the better part of a day and explore this drive filled with wildflowers, lakes, small Texas towns, meadows, and mountains. We had also heard of Lake Travis, which was reputed to be a beautiful lake that had amazing views, homes, and recreation. We saw pictures of its beauty and the many million and multi-million dollar homes that lined the lake. The pictures made it look like a Mediterranean-style getaway.

So, we did the Texas Hill Country drive and had an amazing day. As a side note, we ran across a small town that my wonderful wife had, to my amazement, never heard of. We came to Luckenbach, Texas, which was made famous by Waylon Jennings. She said not only had she never heard of it, she was confident that none of our friends had either, and I was a weirdo. Needless to say, after a couple texts to friends, she realized that she was the one out of touch. We also discovered many other interesting sites along this drive, including the LBJ ranch and museum, small towns with charm to spare, fields of wildflowers, and Lake Travis. However, when we got to Lake Travis, our expected view and our actual view were two completely different things. Indeed, there were the fancy lake homes rimming the lake. However, these homes were a hundred yards from the shore of the lake. Docks, rather than being places to jump off and swim or dock fancy boats, were instead flat on dry ground. The expectation of what we saw in pictures from the internet, compared to the reality of what we saw was stark.

What we didn't know at the time was that this area was in the midst of a historic drought. We also didn't know that Lake Travis was a dammed lake, part of a chain of lakes that fed the valley below it, including Austin. Water was being drained from the lake to meet the electricity needs of the community downriver. Water was being released and diverted to meet the agribusiness needs of the area below as well. Meanwhile, no water was coming into this usually beautiful lake.

I wonder if your relationship with Jesus has ever looked like this dried up picture of Lake Travis. You see, this is what our spiritual lives look like when we aren't experiencing the inflow of Jesus in our lives. When our faith and life are absent of true prayer, diving deep into the Bible, experiencing community with other followers of Jesus, journaling and thinking deeply, and so on, we are suffering from an inflow issue in our faith. As we live and try to serve others, try to meet the needs of others, try to live out our faith, but don't have the power of Jesus enabling us to do these things, our lives look like those pictures of Lake Travis during the drought. Our lives do not look like God intended.

The simple truth is that *we can't give what we don't have.*

One of the most important things that Jesus ever said is in response to a great question. A teacher of the law asked Jesus which was the most important commandment. Jews strived to follow to the letter of the law so much that they even would wear the laws around. I think about the many detailed commands in the book of the law about seemingly every little detail of life. I imagine the teacher looking down at a huge scroll of the law as he earnestly asked Jesus this great question. And I am blown away by the simplicity *and* fullness of Jesus response:

> "Love the Lord your God with all your heart and with all your soul and with all your mind. This is the first and greatest commandment. And the second is like it: Love our neighbor as yourself" (Matt 22:37).

In other words, we need the inflow of God in our lives to really be in a place where we can be loving him with everything. This inflow comes from loving him with all our heart, soul, and mind by seeking him in prayer, scripture, fellowship, journaling, fasting, and whatever other means allow us to draw close to him. I am also struck by the connectedness of the second part of Jesus' statement above.

Let me backtrack to the lake/soul analogy. I have previously talked about the Dead Sea. We learned its shores are 1,412 feet below sea level. It is one of earth's lowest elevations on land. We also talked about the fact that it is almost ten times as salty as the ocean. In fact, it is 34 percent salinity. What I didn't talk about is why it is so saline. The Dead Sea is what is known as a closed body of water. Recall that Lake Stevens had three inflows and one primary outflow. The Dead Sea is fed by the Jordan River, but has no outflows; the only water loss is through evaporation. The lack of outflow makes for the stagnant water, the high salinity, and the lack of life in its waters. The "Dead Sea" certainly has earned its name.

The truth is that our spiritual lives look like the Dead Sea if we have the inflow of God in our lives, but have no outflow. In the words of Jesus above, he sums up that we are to love him with every ounce of everything we have and in turn love others well. That is the basis of our whole faith. We were meant to serve and love others. If we have the inflow of Jesus' love in our lives, but aren't looking to feed the hungry, help the poor, or make disciples of others, we are missing it. Our faith will become stagnant and dead, just like the Dead Sea. James, Jesus' brother, said it this way: "faith by itself, if it is not accompanied by action, is dead" (Jas 2:17)—just like the Dead Sea. To look at the gospel accounts of Jesus is to see this dynamic in his own life. He got away by himself to pray. He fasted. He attended places of worship and teaching. He knew God's word and could quote and apply it whenever he needed. *And* he spent most of his time healing, serving, teaching, and making God's name known.

If we want to make sure we are influencing our community in a way that flows with God's unique purpose for us, we need the inflow of Jesus to turn around and give to others out of the overflow.

I have two more bodies of water to look at before the end of this chapter. Unfortunately, I was unable to get photo permissions for the following lake, but if you were to do a search, you would see a nasty sight. The water hue of the lake is a mix of deep dark red and orange. It looks a bit like a mix of sludge and blood. Abandoned, ominous buildings dot the shore in places. This is reputed to be the most polluted lake in the entire world. It is Lake

Karachay in Russia. For years, nuclear waste was poured directly into the lake. Let me restate that: *nuclear waste* was poured into this fresh water lake. It is said that one cannot stand on the shores more than an hour without certain death. Below is another polluted lake.

In the United States, one of the most polluted lakes is Onondaga Lake, located in New York by Syracuse. For years, a chemical company poured toxic waste into the lake. Additionally, when the sewer system was overwhelmed, raw sewage poured directly into the lake. A picture does not do the pollution justice, as the water is a very unnatural, burnt red hue.

Why would anyone in their right mind pour nuclear waste into a freshwater lake? Or toxic chemical waste, or for that matter, *human* waste? These are all things that just weren't meant to be there.

Likewise, as I desire to be on Mission My Town, and influence the people in my community, I have things in my life at times that just weren't meant to be there. Not only do I want to be spending time with Jesus to have his inflow and influence in my life, as well as looking for the unique way he has for me to serve and love others in my community, he also wants me to guard what is put in the waters of my soul.

We live in an almost impossible time with temptation. The speed and ease of accessing information online, which is a blessing, has also created huge struggle in our battle for purity. We can access pictures, videos, or other content to make it not only easier to learn and grow as a person, but also to allow sin patterns to develop strong footholds in our lives. Culture and society also give very little boundaries on our sexual or covetous lives.

What God desires for us in terms of the way we use our bodies and minds is completely counter-cultural. We don't see until later how giving our hearts and bodies away so freely creates an emptiness and portal to pain. We bring toxic relationships and activities into our lives. In short, we are often like the lakes above.

Officials have tried for years to clean Lake Onondaga. It has been a slow, painful, and largely unsuccessful process. Sometimes dealing with the aftereffects of sin in our lives is much the same.

God has promised us complete forgiveness. He says that as far as the east is from the west, so far has he removed our sin from us. You can't be any further than that. We want to make sure that we are living in the freedom of forgiveness. God has wiped the slate clean.

I look at David of the Old Testament. God called him a "man after my own heart." God ordained him to lead the nation. David was a truly special man who wrote much of the book of Psalms, was a powerful king, and led an amazing life.

He also committed adultery and had the woman's husband killed.

He was completely forgiven and made new.

However, the effects of his sin crippled his leadership, family, and future in ways that he never would have imagined. His kids suffered and David had poor relationships with them for the remainder of his days. His leadership was weakened. The truth was, David was still a man after God's own heart. And the consequences of his disobedience and sin were real.

We all sin and struggle. We won't be perfect. We will struggle in thought and word and action. But the truth is, there are things that just are not meant to be in the life of a follower of Jesus. Just as nuclear, chemical, and human waste are not meant to be in freshwater, the Bible tells us many things that aren't meant to be in our lives.

James 1:27 says: "Religion that God our Father accepts as pure and faultless is this: to look after orphans and widows in their distress and to keep oneself from being polluted by the world." These words simplify faith to action and purity. How challenging these words are!

I know for myself, even as I write this, there are things present in my life that God doesn't want there. I wonder if we would all be so bold as to really examine our lives and look at what God would have us get rid of. What things could be hampering your ability to truly mission to your wife, husband, kids, grandchildren, friends, and coworkers, and are not allowing you to experience the effectiveness that God desires? The real way we miss out is that we don't experience the joy that he wants to give us.

One of my favorite and most convicting verses in the Bible is Proverbs 4:23: "Above all else, *guard your heart*, for it is the wellspring of life" (emphasis added). It is one of my favorites because I have experienced its truth. In seasons of my life, when tempted towards a relationship or habit that would be counter to his best, I have been able to guard my heart against these things. As a result, I have experienced deep joy and communion with the Holy Spirit. Likewise, this verse is one of my most convicting because I have experienced its truth in other ways. I have held onto relationships that God wanted me to end or alter. I have kept hidden habits or thoughts that he wanted me to guard against. The truth is that whether things are good or bad, whichever we allow to enter and grow in our hearts give life to the thoughts and actions we experience. Sin patterns that entangle us and ensnare us are almost always the result of not guarding our hearts well and allowing "waste" to enter our waters.

Before we move ahead in our quest to fully live out this Mission My Town, I wonder if you are taking the time to reflect and journal on the questions I have listed at the end of each chapter or, better yet, those that God may be asking you. I feel that the reflection questions at the end of this chapter are especially important if you want to be what God wants you to be.

JOURNAL AND REFLECTION QUESTIONS:

1. Am I experiencing the inflow of Jesus in my life through time with him in prayer, Scripture, fellowship, journaling, fasting, or other means? If not, what is holding me back?

2. Am I experiencing the outflow of God's love through me to others? Do I have a means to give away my faith? Do I have a ministry that I am involved in that allows me to take this love for Jesus and help create this love in others?

3. Are my waters clean? Have I not guarded my heart against something that I now need to take a stand against?

8

Sighting Your Target

HAVE YOU EVER MISSED something completely obvious? I am sometimes the opposite of Captain Obvious. I don't know how many times Lori has talked about observing something that I had been looking at for weeks and never noticed. This trait certainly hasn't helped my cause at times with a wife that loves a clean, organized house when I don't even notice the clutter. As a coach, after one particular game, my assistant coaches and players were excitedly talking about a fight that took place in the stands during the second half of a game. I hadn't even noticed. Despite the fact that a quarter of the section of fans apparently cleared out, punches were thrown, and people gathered around the fighters as it happened, I didn't notice, because, well, the game was going on. And I am oblivious sometimes.

One such time happened as I was driving through my community and pulled to a stoplight. As I mindlessly listened to the radio and looked at wet brake lights in front of me, I looked to the right and had a moment of clarity. My eyes locked on the Target store logo and I suddenly noticed for the first time that it was actually a *target*. Don't ask me how, but somehow for all these years, I had missed that this wasn't a random collection of concentric circles but was actually the shape of a "target." Wow.

This story does remind me of the truth that many people are going through their lives without their own targets. Many people are getting up, eating breakfast, going to school/work, getting in a workout or watching their kids' games, eating dinner, doing more work on their computer (with many moments of social media mixed in throughout), going to bed tired, and doing the whole thing again the next day. Many people are counting the days and not really making their days count.

One of the best gifts we can give God, ourselves, and the people around us is the gift of thinking deeply and often about our purpose. Most of us could use the commitment to spend more time being *intentional* about our days and not simply letting them unfold, hoping that we are on the path that God has set for us and that we are impacting the people God intends for us to impact. One thing that has helped our family to live *for* purpose, *on* purpose is the creation of our family mission statement.

I can see your eye rolls from here as I write this. I myself have sat through work meetings designed to create the perfect mission statement that defines our business and work. I also know the mind-numbing process that this can be with people arguing over word choice, purpose, goals, and so on before you end up with a five-paragraph mission statement that is often more confusing than clarifying.

Lori and I have always had a mission statement as a couple. It is something that we either were challenged to do or prompted to do early in our lives together. It was a great way to make sure that we were on the same page. It was also a great filter for doing activities and making commitments that either did or did not meet the filter of our mission statement. It was something that we could revisit from time to time to make sure that what we were doing with our life together was actually what we felt God had compelled us to do.

The process of having a family mission statement needed to be revisited as we had kids and then again as they got older. A couple of years ago, we began with a family motto and used it often in our homes, communicated it a lot with our kids, and even asked them every once in a while if they could recite it.

Then, one day as my son, Max, recited it, I realized our wording emphasized wrong priorities and needed to be modified. At the time it was: "We are the Hein's, we work hard, play hard, love God, and serve others." As Max said it, I was stung by conviction. As you probably have figured out, Lori and I are plagued by workaholism and over-commitment. Even as I write this book, I am the head coach of two sports, teach AP classes at our high school, am pursuing my National Board certification in teaching, helping coach Max's basketball team, and leading Wyldlife for our kids and their friends. So, as Max started with, "We are the Hein's, we work hard," I realized that we were doing our kids and our God a disservice by this being the first phrase. We have since rephrased our family mission statement to more accurately reflect what we want our lives and family to be about in our community.

As one walks into our living room, there is this sign hanging prominently on the wall.

This simple family motto has served many purposes. It defines what we want to be known for in our town. It helps us create lessons for our kids about what it means to be on mission together. It serves as a reminder and sometimes a strong conviction when we are missing the mark in one of these areas. It reminds me personally to take the time and have fun, laugh, and play. We even sometimes ask each other at the dinner table which of these we were able to experience that day.

Another story that I have actually never told anyone until this writing is an embarrassing moment I've kept to myself. I wonder if you have ever had a similar experience. We moved to Lake Stevens about fifteen years ago. Previously we had been living in Spokane, Washington. These towns are separated by about a five-and-a-half hour drive. When we first moved, I have to admit, it was hard sometimes to remember which place was home. Do I call Spokane "home" even though I have moved and don't really feel like Lake Stevens is my home? And vice versa. Early on, as we were making the transition from one community to the other, I spent many hours driving between the two.

On one occasion, we hadn't yet moved, but I was going to Lake Stevens to coach a summer tournament. Like any mere mortal, Mother Nature was calling and I stopped after a few hours. I took my time, got some lunch and got back on the road. My mind immediately started spinning many different directions: should we really buy a house yet? Should we really have sold our house on our own? Is Lori truly on board with this move? Did I hear God correctly in taking this job and making this move? What offense was going to really fit the skillset and athleticism of these guys? Question after question flooded my mind.

With my mind on autopilot, I drove the familiar stretch of road. It was a hot summer day and I had my window rolled down, a good CD in (remember when we actually used those), and my mind rolling a hundred miles an hour in different directions. As I sped by wheat fields, sagebrush, crossed a bridge over the Columbia river, and passed through a couple small towns, I thought about how familiar this road had become on my travels.

Then my mind caught up with my reality and I had a sudden awareness. Part of the reason this road was so familiar was that I had been traveling on it the past few hours. In the opposite direction. Going the other way. I suddenly realized that, as my mind had been preoccupied, my thoughts concerned about the future and past I couldn't control, I had been speeding for over an hour in the direction I had just come from. I suddenly saw John Candy in "Planes, Trains, and Automobiles" laughing and scoffing as someone yelled at him, "You're going the wrong way!" I had indeed been absent-mindedly going the wrong way for over an hour.

Wherever you are in life, I don't want you to be guilty of absentmindedly "going the wrong way." Whether you are a single mom, college junior, retired grandparent, millennial, or baby boomer, I encourage you to set a personal or family motto. In the words often attributed to Socrates: "The unexamined life is not worth living." This is possibly a bit harsh, but there may be a lot of truth to it. We want to listen to God, to our passions, to our gifts and abilities, to our experiences. We want to notice where God has placed us and what he wants us to do there. A personal motto or mission statement is a great place to start.

Remember the Circle of Intention activity with the Venn Diagrams? Did you take the time to fill in your circles? For your sake and for getting the most out of our time together, I would encourage you to go back and do this if you didn't. The next part of our journey over the next several chapters is to closely look at the circles that many of us have in common. Let's dig in!

JOURNAL AND REFLECTION QUESTIONS:

1. Do you have a mission statement for you or your family? If no, why not? If so, does it still apply to your station in life?

2. If your answer was no above, I encourage you to take some real time to develop one. Pray. Ask God for what he wants your life to be about. Journal. Have real conversation with your family if applicable.

3. We will now begin looking more specifically at our Circles of Intention. If you didn't complete the activity earlier in the book on this topic, please do so now.

9

People at the End of the Tunnel

CIRCLE OF INTENTION: OUR HOME

I HAVE HAD A profession that is somewhat humorous when you sit back and look at it. I have been a basketball coach for over twenty-five years. My experiences have spanned being a college assistant coach, high school assistant coach, and a head high school basketball coach for twenty years. It is eye-opening to sit back and look at how all parties involved (including myself) lose sight of the fact that we are talking about the ability of a group of sixteen- and seventeen-year-old boys to coordinate and put a spherical ball through an iron ring. It is eye-opening that most parents care much more about how many minutes their son plays on a Friday night, than they do about his second period trigonometry class. As a coach, it is sad that I lose more sleep over a tough loss in a basketball game to a league rival than I do to hearing of hunger in my community or the fact that homelessness is still a problem in the county in which I live. We live with probably far too much passion and emphasis on a game. Nevertheless, it is a huge passion in my life and the passions of our fans is real as well.

Some of my career highlights have been seeing the "People at the End of the Tunnel." In 2009, our school had the opportunity to take a team to the AAAA state tournament for the first time in school history, and the first opportunity to go to state in twenty-seven years. The 2009 season was a great journey in which we overcame many hardships and earned the community's admiration. Our hard-working, defensive-minded group earned the community's following. We were picked as the lowest of the sixteen teams in the state tournament, but the team went on to overachieve, playing three teams that finished the season in the state's top five rankings. One of our highlights was seeing the "People at the End of the Tunnel" after our third day in the tournament.

That day we played Eisenhower High, a team who had a great season, a hall of fame coach, and was ranked in the top couple of teams throughout the entire year. We had a great game and it ended with our best player at the free throw line with two shots and 1.4 seconds on the clock, down one point. The first free throw hit probably every single square inch of the rim and fell through the hoop. Our player at the line had a huge sigh of relief, as did every member of our fan contingency. As the second free throw swished through the rim and a half-court heave was well off the mark, it meant the first placing trophy in a long time for our school. We celebrated in the locker room and there was a feeling of so much joy. The guys dressed and we all headed out of the locker room. The old facility where the tournament is held requires a walk through an old hallway, then out from under the bleachers into the dome. We took the walk and found the People at the End of the Tunnel.

Hundreds of people from the community were there to congratulate us, pat us on the back, give hugs, and celebrate this moment with us. The People at the End of the Tunnel were so happy to share in our victory and to congratulate the guys. It was a very moving experience for me as a coach, since we had worked very hard to build a culture of success in basketball. However, it was even more meaningful because I have seen both sides of the fence of human approval. My wife and I hugged in this tumult of people and emotion.

We had the good fortune of having some very good teams over a several year period. In particular, we had a very high winning percentage at home for a five-year span. We had seasons where we were undefeated on our home court, and only lost maybe one game at home all year. It was a place where people lingered after games. Typically, my young kids ran around the floor with other kids after the finish and then people lingered in the hallway right outside of our locker room, waiting for the team to come back out through the tunnel to the hallway immediately outside the gym. I typically hugged my wife and kissed my kids goodnight, as I still had details to tie up.

The following season in 2010 we were in a neck-and-neck race with a rival school for the second year in a row, dueling for the league title. Late in the game, we were up three points with only a few seconds remaining. We fouled one of their worst free throw shooters, who had a one-on-one opportunity. This is certainly a scenario where we had the statistical advantage. The player rattled in the first free throw, then missed the second one badly on purpose. The ball came off the rim very hard and bounced off three different pairs of hands before being misdirected wildly into the hands of their best three-point shooter who caught, released, and swished the ball as the buzzer sounded.

It was a crazy scene: the gym went from a loud frenzy, rocking with the band playing, fans cheering, and so on, to sudden complete silence from our home crowd. It was as if the air suddenly drained from the facility. It was one of the toughest finishes to a game that I have coached. A few minutes later I found myself addressing a stunned group of guys, trying to make sense of what had happened. They filed out, I spoke with my assistants briefly, then headed out the tunnel. As I came through the tunnel, it was a moment that will forever remain with me.

The only People at the End of the Tunnel were my wife and two kids.

It was a stunning reminder of many things at all once. It was a reminder that you tend to be more supported and better received when you have worldly success. It was good accountability to me that maybe I am unapproachable after losing. But the moment was rich in truth that the people who really matter most to me were these people there for me at the end of the tunnel. This phrase the "People at the End of the Tunnel" has continued to be my phrase for keeping the priorities right, keeping my family number 1, not number 1a, as my important people.

Why do I share this with you now? It is simple. As I began to really pursue what God had for me in my circles of intention, I found myself busy, trying to meet the needs of many people and feeling pulled in many directions. I was striving to Mission My Town, sometimes doing it as Jesus wanted, sometimes not. But I found myself once again swept away in busyness, overactivity, and every-night commitments. Simultaneously, we had some behaviors happening in our kids that were concerning.

Lori and I struggled to make sense of some of the behaviors that the kids seemed to be struggling with. As we searched for answers found in the kids' personalities or unique adoption history, we had a painful realization. In our pursuit of everything else, we were losing sight of prioritizing the

People at the End of the Tunnel. Nights of turning the iPads and laptops back on after dinner to do more work; nights of events for other people; time spent with our kids but not really *with* them—time spent with them but thinking about other things that needed to get done.

Sometimes we can neglect the best for the good. Sometimes we can miss the chance to dwell on the most important things in our life while striving to take care of one hundred other very important things. Our heart is to keep Jesus first, keep our family second, and keep the mission of our community third.

If you are married or hope to be married, I have a thought for you. If your marriage is not strong and not grounded in the model of the Bible, your parenting will suffer, your ministry will suffer, and ultimately your mission in your town will suffer. I have seen so many parents put their kids above their marriage. A wise counselor once told me that more than anything, what my kids need from me is to see me love their mom well. Kids find tremendous security in seeing genuine love between their parents. If you are on a ministry team and are preaching love, your team and followers will dismiss you in a second if they don't first see that love in you, for your spouse.

What your kids need most is quite possibly to see that you really love your spouse deeply and well. This is the parenting gift that "keeps on giving." It creates safety in their lives. It impacts their view of love, relationships, and even God. A devoted, committed, if not always perfect, marriage will give them a model down the road to navigate their own relationships, and possibly marriages with commitment.

The truth is, having a high priority, committed, loving marriage is hard. And fun. And rewarding. And what God intended it to be. Some people describe a good marriage as a 50/50 proposition. Lori and I have found that our marriage looks and feels like it was most intended when we treat it 100/100. A 50/50 relationship is *transactional*. Your mindset can become, "I am going to stop giving my 50 percent because the other person clearly isn't living up to his or her 50 percent." We can get caught "keeping score" of the way our needs are met or unmet. Love becomes entitlement; we may refuse to give our end of the bargain, or at least give it resentfully, if we view our partner as not giving their 50 percent. A 100/100 relationship is more *transformational*. You are committing everything you have to your marriage and to your spouse. You don't have to worry about keeping score, because you are more concerned about giving your spouse what they need than you are your own needs. You become a student of your spouse. You understand their "love language." You work to understand what brings them great joy, as well as what brings them embarrassment, sadness, or lack of fulfillment.

Have you been to many weddings? Chances are, if you are a young adult or older, you have been to some weddings. Many that I have been to use the following scripture from 1 Corinthians 13:

> "Love is patient, love is kind. It does not envy, it does not boast, it is not proud. It does not dishonor others, it is not self-seeking, it is not easily angered, it keeps no record of wrongs. Love does not delight in evil but rejoices with the truth. It always protects, always trusts, always hopes, always perseveres."

I think a daily homework assignment for those of us that love another would be to read these words and see how we are doing toward our partner on the Bible's definition of love. These works strike me: "Love is not self-seeking; it keeps no record of wrongs." If you are in a 100/100 relationship it is almost impossible to be self-seeking or to make a list of your partner's wrongdoings.

Many people in our town know "Mark." Many people know "Lori." And many know "Mark and Lori." We, like many of you, are a plural to many around us. What we have discovered is that our marriage holds one of our greatest ministry opportunities. As previously stated, our own kids are watching us carefully. We have their friends in our house all the time for sleepovers and hangouts. These kids are also watching us. Many people in our community know us as a couple as well, and we believe that God gave us to each other to enhance the joy and purpose in each other's lives. We also believe God put us together for others. We hope that the way we love and treat each other, the way we partner together for God's causes, the way we are each other's biggest fans and support in the things we do "separately," all serve to make a statement about Jesus Christ.

Some of you who are reading this book are unmarried. You may desire never to get married. However, many of you are hopeful that God brings you someone down the road (or now). These words are for you. I am going to get very real here.

Are you treating dating relationships and physical boundaries with your future spouse in mind? Are you careful with the dating relationships you enter, as they will impact your future spouse? A 100/100 relationship with someone you haven't even met would be putting the needs of this potential spouse into consideration. It also would entail looking at God's design in the Bible. I find it so interesting that people look at God as the "fun police." They think that the Bible is set up to make us feel guilty and to take away any fun we can have. However, I believe that God gives us his wisdom to create *joy*. We may give up some things that the world takes as "normal" so that we can have much more joy and fulfillment in our marital relationships.

Sin is sin. Sin separates us from God and the joy we can find in life by living closely with him. Some of us are experiencing this lack of closeness with Jesus because we are making decisions that rob us of joy. Even though all sin separates us from God, sexual sin is unique in the way it is so personal and is a misuse of one of God's greatest gifts that was meant to show intimacy with our spouse and spouse only. Paul says that "all other sins a person commits are outside of his body, but whoever sins sexually sins against their own body" (1 Cor 6:18). Our sexuality is one of the greatest gifts we can share with our spouse or future spouse. It is a big deal to God because he doesn't want us to miss out on the joy someday of this part of our relationship with our spouse.

I want to challenge you if you are unmarried: *wait*. As someone who had the honor of marrying someone who waited, it is an amazing thing to know that this person waited for *you*. It is God's design for a reason. Despite what culture and the "locker room" would tell you, people *do* wait. I and several of my close friends chose to wait. There are people out there. I realize that I am offending some of you, but I am just asking you to consider God's plan for your sexual life and the joy he wants to bring you. Why would God design it for me to wait? Let's think about some of the things that people deal with when they don't wait. The possibility and reality of disease. The very real possibility of having a child before you or your relationship is ready. Giving yourself away and then realizing you were being used. Wondering about what comparisons your partner might be making. The list goes on. God wants to give you joy.

What if I am already past that decision? What if I have already given myself to someone sexually? What if I am living with someone right now? How do I go backward? God is more full of grace than we could ever imagine. One of my favorite accounts of Jesus' grace is in John 8.

Jesus was up early and as the sun rose over the Mount of Olives, he walked into the temple, where people were already gathered. People grouped around him and a buzz filled the air as this teacher, who taught so differently than their Jewish leaders, sat down. People settled in and sat down on all sides of Jesus as he began to teach them. The modern-day equivalent is you sitting down in church, Starbucks in hand, ready to listen to your favorite pastor.

Suddenly, the doors flung open, and commotion entered the room. The peaceful teaching atmosphere was suddenly broken by the sound of yelling and wrestling, and a group of teachers of the law and Pharisees entered the room dragging a woman caught in the act of adultery. I imagine she hardly had time to get her clothes back on; after all, she was caught "in the act." I can almost imagine the pain and embarrassment in her eyes, her torn clothes and messy hair as they pushed her in front of Jesus, demanding action. In keeping with the law of the times, she was to be taken outside, have people gather around her and throw rocks and stones at her until she died. My, how times have changed. I also wonder what kind of society did this to women, while there was no mention or repercussion for the man involved. I imagine the look of disdain, anger, self-righteousness etched on the faces of these preachers and teachers adorned in fancy shawls and robes with intricate detailing. They were also hoping to catch Jesus in a trap, wondering how he would balance the law with the love they had already seen in watching him.

I love Jesus even more every time I read this story and see his response to sin, in this case sexual sin. Jesus at first reacted in the strangest way. He bent down and began to write with his finger in the dirt on the temple floor. The Bible doesn't say why, but I have my opinions. Imagine being there. Jesus bends down and begins writing; what would you do? Wouldn't the natural response be to lean in, try to get a view of what Jesus is doing? People were wondering what in the world he would write. In my mind, his action if full of grace. This immediately took the focus off the woman in their midst with the torn clothes and certain death sentence. Jesus wrote in the sand and people began to put their focus on him. I imagine him doodling for a full minute or two, a quiet settling back across the commotion, waiting for his response. It is awesome.

Slowly the Pharisees began to question him again. "What should be done to her? She was caught sinning sexually!" I see Jesus slowly stand up and the crowd take a step back to see what happens next. Jesus looks slowly from Pharisee to Pharisee, staring them directly in the eye. They quiet down and Jesus then completes the transition of the attention going from the woman, to him, and now to them.

"Let any one of you who is without sin be the first to throw a stone at her."

With one sentence, he summons more wisdom, grace, compassion, and conviction than I could have ever have created with ten thousand words. The self-righteous Pharisees evidently felt the same, as did the crowd. Jesus knelt back down and began to draw in the dirt and sand again.

The Bible tells us that, slowly, people began to go away, one at a time. Interestingly, it says they went away, the "older ones first." If Jesus told me this, I would walk away as well. I have lived long enough to know I have sinned many ways and many times. I would be in no place to throw a stone. Everyone realized the same and, after a time, the only people left were Jesus, hunched over, drawing on the temple floor, and the partially clothed woman, standing and shivering in shame.

At this point, Jesus stands up and asks her, "Woman, where are they? Has no one condemned you?" She looks tentatively, and hopefully, into Jesus' eyes, "No one, sir." Then the words that must have changed her soul, "Then neither do I condemn you." Amazing, amazing grace. This is the Jesus that I love so much. However, he adds one more sentence that also is indicative of what he desires not only for this woman, but also for us who are trapped in sexual sin of any kind.

"Go now and leave your life of sin."

What does this mean for you? Do you need to stop pursuing that girl who you know doesn't walk with Jesus? Do you need to end the relationship with the guy who is toxic and you know in your heart is not God's best? Do you need to stop sleeping with your fiancé and begin to honor God anew together? Do you need to stop living together, move out, and begin to honor God here as well? Are you married yet have thoughts or even actions for another person? Are you married or unmarried and have a problem with pornography that you think is your secret battle? The obvious lie we tell ourselves is that pornography or hidden sexual sin is hidden. God knows. He sees all. And it stifles the Holy Spirit and therefore the work of God in your heart and life. It impacts your relationship with Jesus. It will also impact your future relationship with your spouse. So, what would Jesus tell you? Probably the same thing he told the woman brought before him. "Go and leave your life of sin." The truth is that if pornography is an issue in your life, it will impact your Mission My Town. It will rob you of your personal joy and effectiveness to live out your faith.

Heavy stuff, but worth the fight. Don't wait to ask for God's forgiveness. Perhaps even confess to a very trusted friend and ask for some accountability and support. Look at using some type of tool, such as Covenant Eyes, to help you in your struggle. Most people think they are in this struggle alone. You certainly are not. Most people think it is no big deal. It is. Purity matters very much to God because it impacts his relationship with you and his ability to work through you. Enter the fray; make a change. Have the courage to ask for forgiveness and ask for help.

Some of you may have kids as your People at the End of the Tunnel. You might not have kids, but you may have nieces or nephews. You might have kids that you mentor or care for deeply. Possibly you have kids and grandkids. This is one of the most precious Circles of Intention you could have.

Recently, we were at a church when the youth pastor, Trevor, was speaking on his theme "Don't miss it." Do you ever have that moment in church when the pastor says something you swear is *just for you*. The way it is said, the timing of what is said, the complete way it resonates with where you are. Well, this was one of those times. Someone—it may have been yours truly—was grouchy, trying to get preteens moving and out the door in time to be very late. I spoke harshly to Max. I quieted my daughter, McKaden, with a sharp, sarcastic quip. And now, my back straightened and my eyes widened as Trevor shared that on average we have about one thousand weeks with our kids from the time they are born to the time they leave us. I suddenly did some math and realized that we had less than that due to the fact that we had adopted our amazing kids at the ages of one and three.

"Don't miss it." Don't miss this time you have to mold and enjoy your kids. Sometimes we rationalize missing so much for the sake of providing. There certainly are those seasons where work is tough to come by or is inflexible. To make ends meet we do the best we can with the circumstances we're given. However, I am also convinced, based on my own selfishness and lack of perspective, that there are many times I could organize my life differently to be more available to my kids. I don't know your situation and the last thing I truly want to do is judge you in this. If you do need conviction, God will provide it.

Truth be told, Lori and I are both workers. We love hard work, we enjoy the work to which we have been called. And we both sometimes abuse work. Sometimes my profession can also become my obsession. Sometimes during the winter, my mind never really stops. If I have "dead space" or time between engaged thinking or involvement in something, my mind imme-diately seeks to overcome the Rubik's Cube of work-related issues. For me, it might be how to attack the match-up zone of our rival high school. It might be how to better utilize our best shooter or post-up player. It might be how to better reach that senior who seems to be struggling with confi-dence. The list goes on. I have become better about rearranging my time and commitments and being present more frequently. But in my presence, I am not always *present*.

Truth and transparency—brutally honest here. There have been more than several times I have been snuggled up with my kids, eating popcorn, watching some animated animal sing and dance once again, or watching some dragon fly a nasally boy on its back, where my mind is in full-on work mode. There may or may not have been a time or two when physically I was trying to buy Boardwalk or Park Place as I was moving my little silver car, but mentally, I was creating a tennis or basketball practice plan in my mind. Many of the things that distract us away from our kids will still be there when our kids are long gone. And even if they won't be, they certainly aren't worth compromising our relationship with our kids.

"Don't miss it." Don't miss your role. You, and uniquely you, have a role to play in your kids' spiritual and personal development that nobody else can play. It is very true that every child needs another caring adult telling them the same things a loving parent would. Our kids need other strong adults. But nobody can replace a parent's God-given role in their lives. This is not intended to be a parenting book. However, here are a few thoughts on the things your kids might need at various stages. Are they pre-school age? *Embrace* them. Physically and emotionally embrace them and let them know early on that they are safe and deeply loved. Elementary kids need you to *engage*. They want assurance you know and care for what they like. Really work to get to know what makes them special and unique and engage in understanding the things your kids love. Middle schoolers need *affirmation*. Between puberty, pimples, first crushes, braces, regrettable haircuts, and fashion trends, middle school is tough sledding for even the most well-adjusted of us. They need to know you love, and possibly even more importantly, *like* who they are. High schoolers need a lot of things. Primarily they need you to help *mobilize* them. Help them learn how to be responsible, make strong choices, move toward some goals after high school. From what I understand from my mentors, once kids are past these stages, it is still important for us to fill these needs at various times.

As we wrap this chapter up, I challenge you to realize that your People at the End of the Tunnel are the Circle that really matters. If you are successful in all the other circles, but miss the mark on this one, it will leave much sadness for the people you love the most. Make sure we "major on the majors" and keep perspective that these People at the End of the Tunnel matter more than all the people we see in the stands of our community. Your ministry will be hollow to your kids looking up to you and your spouse looking to you if you neglect them for others' sake.

JOURNAL AND REFLECTION QUESTIONS:

1. Who would you define as your People at the End of the Tunnel?

2. If married: what is the quality of your commitment to your spouse right now? If unmarried, yet have a desire to one day be married: how are you doing with choices that one day could impact your spouse?

3. If you have kids, grandkids, nephews, nieces, etc: reflect on ways you are loving them well. Reflect on what God might be saying to you in terms of loving them even better.

4. What safeguards have you put in place in your life to counteract "hidden" sin? What might you need to do further?

10

Less Than Perfect

CIRCLE OF INTENTION: EXTENDED FAMILY

DO YOU EVER JUST think about the craziness that was the life of Jesus? I know we read the stories in the gospels and think about them. But do you ever really try to visualize what it would have been like to be a first-hand observer to the crazy train that was Jesus' years of ministry? Really, who has seen anyone control the weather? Heal a blind man or a leper? Change water into wine? Get affirmed by a voice from heaven as he was baptized?! Get transfigured on a mountain? (Let alone raise people from the dead and be raised from death himself.) Visualize any one of those.

Jesus was powerful and perfect; the Bible assures us of that. Our faith hinges on the fact that he was both God and human. John uses elegant, culturally and historically significant language to assure us that Jesus was the "Word," the Greek word "Logos," which held deep significance for people of the day. He goes on to say that "the Word was with God, and the Word was God" (John 1:1). He then tells us that "the Word became flesh and made his dwelling among us" (John 1:14). Literally, Jesus was God with skin on. He was so powerful and beyond wise. He loved people in a way that shattered people's viewpoint of religion or even the concept of love. He brought healing to situations that were beyond repair. He changed the world, history, and people's lives more than anyone before or since. He was perfect.

But even his family didn't believe in Jesus.

This is one of the great mind-benders of the Bible for me. It also gives me some peace and hope for family relationships that aren't perfect. In his perfection, Jesus dealt with imperfect people and relationships even in his own home.

Do you have a father or a mother who doesn't know Jesus? Maybe you carry the pain of having an aging parent or grandparent who has little to no relationship with you or even God. It is possible that you have a sibling you haven't spoken to in years. There might be a deep hurt that time just doesn't seem to heal. There might be relationships and situations in your family that seem well beyond hope. You might even be in a place to not even care, let alone hope, that these relationships will ever be restored.

It is said that the holidays are some of the most painful times of the year for many people. Some experience forced conversations with someone they know really doesn't like or approve of them. It may take the form of awkward silence at the dinner table, realizing that those gathered have blood and genetics in common, but virtually nothing else. There might be some real wounds that a holiday ham just isn't going to cure. I realize the bad pun even as I write that last sentence. Our family and relatives are going to bring us much joy and, correspondingly, much possible pain.

In the Bible, John 7:5 says about Jesus, "For even his own brothers did not believe in him." Even in his perfection, he experienced the imperfect in his family. It isn't hard to visualize Jesus' brothers developing some animosity toward him. I am imagining conversations in his father's carpentry shop, "Why can't you be more like Jesus?" For those of us with older siblings, it is hard enough to live up to the positives of these imperfect people. Imagine having a brother who never sinned. I don't think any of us are in any danger of that!

By most estimates Jesus started his traveling ministry when he was about thirty years old. So, he had already lived with his brothers for many years. He now left the house, and they still didn't believe in him. I can only imagine how difficult that would have been for him to walk through life on the path that God had for him, loving these brothers with a perfect love, and having them not recognize he was the Christ. We are called to do the same. Even if we have unsaved siblings or family, the best we can do is the best we can do. Pray hard. Live out our faith in mistakes and successes. Love these family members the best we know how, while leaning into the wisdom and power of the Bible and the Holy Spirit. Like any other person, we are not the ones that can make a spiritual decision for them. God gave us free will. We cannot control, nor should we try to control, someone else's free will.

Jesus died without his brothers believing in him. He lived his whole earthly life without seeing them come to know him as the Savior. We may or may not be called to the same thing. For Jesus, he hung on the cross facing his death, not seeing his brothers recognize him as the Son of God.

But a beautiful thing happens in Acts 1. If you read too quickly, you might miss it. If you don't know the backstory you might hear it, but not realize the significance. It is one of those verses that brings a smile to my face. Jesus had died and risen. He gave his great commission and then "was taken up before their very eyes, and a cloud hid him from their sight." Shortly after this, his disciples and several other people were together to make sense of all that had happened and was happening. It is here that this verse occurs. "They all joined together constantly in prayer, along with the women and Mary the mother of Jesus, *and with his brothers*" (Acts 1:14). They finally got it! They finally realized that Jesus was indeed the real deal. He was who he claimed to be, and they owned it for themselves.

You and I just never can know how we are impacting others in our extended and immediate families. But we are called to be in it for the long haul, for the duration.

It is so encouraging to look at the life of one of Jesus' brothers, James. He not only believed, he became the leader of the Jerusalem church. As one reads through the book of Acts, you see James become a strong leader who looks for the good in people and worked hard to spread his brother Jesus' mission. Paul even recognized James, Peter, and John as "those reputed to be pillars" (Gal 2:9). He became a man of tremendous influence in the early church.

James also wrote the book of James in the Bible. He has given us the "gift that keeps on giving," which is the Bible. In James we find verses that bring many of us great comfort and/or challenge:

> "Consider it pure joy, my brothers and sisters, whenever you face trials of many kinds, because you know that the testing of your faith develops perseverance. Perseverance must finish its work so that you may be mature and complete, not lacking anything" (Jas 1:2–4).

> "Everyone should be quick to listen, slow to speak and slow to become angry, for man's anger does not bring about the righteous life that God desires" (Jas 1:19–20).

Do not merely listen to the word, and so deceive yourselves. Do what it says" (Jas 1:22).

"Religion that God our Father accepts as pure and faultless is this: to look after orphans and widows in their distress and to keep oneself from being polluted from the world" (Jas 1:27).

"Speak and act as those who are going to be judged by the law that gives freedom, because judgment without mercy will be shown to anyone who has not been merciful. Mercy triumphs over judgment!" (Jas 2:12–13).

"What good is it, my brothers, if a man claims to have faith but has no deeds? Can such faith save him. . .faith, by itself, if it is not accompanied by action, is dead" (Jas 2:14–17).

"But the wisdom that comes from heaven is first of all pure; then peace-loving, considerate, submissive, full of mercy and good fruit, impartial and sincere" (Jas 3:17).

"Submit yourselves, then, to God. Resist the devil, and he will flee from you. Come near to God and he will come near to you" (Jas 4:7).

One can picture James writing these words as he now reflects upon the life of the brother that he lost, but really gained. These powerful challenges and pieces of wisdom are evidences of his observing Jesus for so many years and seeing what faith was really about. I am sure that even as he sat down to write these words, the words and actions of Jesus resonated in his mind and memory.

Let's pray to have this type of impact on those in our families that don't know Jesus.

However, there is still pain in family relationships where both parties might know Jesus. Even in healthy families, there are rifts, misunderstandings, slights, and hurts that can last for years. The old adage is true: "Where you have people, you also will have problems"—and so it probably is with your extended family. It is quite probable there is someone in your extended family with whom you just can't seem to get it right. Maybe you walk on eggshells around them. Possibly, you are downright hostile or cold to each other. Maybe there is something they have said or done in the past that you just can't get past, no matter how hard you try. Some of these relationships just seem beyond repair or even hope.

If you have lived long enough you have known people who are estranged from a family member for years until they get news of a terminal illness, a car crash, a heart attack, a life-altering event. There is story after story of people who then make peace with their loved ones when they are facing the end of their days. Looking death in the eye has a way of bringing perspective to everything. We suddenly realize what is really, truly important and the triviality of other things in which we place so much stock. People suddenly realize that hanging on to that bitterness is not as important as making things right.

Imagine a backpack. Seriously, get it in mind. Maybe you pictured a backpack you use as a student to carry your books. Maybe you are an avid hiker and you pictured the latest and greatest from REI. Whatever form it took, imagine it on your back. Imagine walking along and picking up five or ten pound weights that you place in the backpack. After a period of time, you can imagine this backpack is now starting to hurt your shoulders. The load is highly uncomfortable, even downright painful. This is what bitterness is like. Bitterness is a heavy backpack that only you carry. You pick up slight after slight from your loved one and store it in the backpack of bitterness, never stopping to unload the heavy baggage. Oftentimes, the other person doesn't even know that you are carrying this weight, yet you continue to let it burden you for years.

Enough is enough. Let today be the day that you do everything in *your* power to make wrongs right. Father Time is undefeated. You never know how many days you or your loved one has left. Don't waste time or chances to make things right. As Paul says in Romans 12:18, "If it is possible, *as far as it depends on you*, live at peace with everyone." Be the bigger person if necessary. Take the awkward or even painful risk of facing these situations head-on.

I got to know an older man who lived in the town where I grew up. He lived an uncomplicated life of farming, loving his wife, raising kids, and working hard at his friendships. I had a chance to work for him and he taught me many things while we worked together on a farm outside of a small Eastern Washington town. One thing that I learned slowly was that he was a cycle-breaker.

"Cycle-breaker" is a term I use for someone that changes the trajectory of his or her family. I didn't realize fully until we were talking years later that he faced the divorce of his parents. He faced divorce and discord in the second marriages of his parents. This now elderly man had seen betrayal and alcoholism in his home. He saw physical violence between his parents. And these were all extensions of what his parents had seen and experienced as kids as well. Fast-forward to what his own kids experienced: a still imperfect father, but one who loved them and loved his wife fiercely. They have been married over fifty years and she is still the greatest love of his life. To my knowledge, none of his kids' marriages has the themes of betrayal, physical abuse, or substance abuse, and from the outside, I see beautiful, thriving marriages.

I am very proud of one of my basketball players for his desire to be a cycle-breaker. He recently showed up with a new tattoo. I love tats and the stories behind them, so I asked him about it. He was hesitant at first but picked up steam as he realized I cared and had taken the time to get to know the backstory of his relationship with his dad. His father had largely abandoned him and certainly disappointed him. He explained his tattoo of the tree with roots and other details. The roots represented his family name that he couldn't escape and were part of his story. The strong, vibrant tree growing from these roots represented that he wanted to change his family trajectory. "I want to be the one to bring honor to our family name." I couldn't have been prouder of this kid; he wasn't looking to make excuses, but was looking to make changes.

I wonder if you need to be the cycle-breaker of your family, immediate or extended. Maybe God is calling you to be the one who changes the trajectory of the lives of your own kids, grandchildren, nieces, or nephews by being bold and courageous enough to break the cycles that might exist in your family tree. I believe God would be telling you the same thing he told Joshua.

Joshua, the son of Nun, was undertaking a huge task. The people of Israel had been wandering in a desert for forty years. The trip should have taken less than two weeks. So, it was very unsuccessful from a utilization of time perspective. Additionally, there was constant bickering and discord among the people. They had constantly doubted God, even though they saw more miracles than any generation in the history of the world. They had complained to God, about God, about each other, about the leadership, about . . . well, everything. I don't feel envy for a man tasked with taking over the leadership of this people.

God knew this and told Joshua several times, "Be strong and courageous, for you shall bring the people of Israel into the land I swore to give them. I will be with you" (Josh 1:6). Maybe you are the one similarly tasked by God: be strong and courageous to change *or* continue the leadership of your family into the next generation. Maybe your task looks like Joshua's:

relational unrest and discord, people wasting years changing things that should have been done a long time ago.

Be a cycle-breaker. Be strong and courageous. Remember, God has already promised his presence: "I will be with you."

JOURNAL AND REFLECTION QUESTIONS:

1. What is your most difficult relationship in your family or extended family? Journal on this and whether God would have you do anything beyond what you have previously done to make peace.

2. Do you have anyone in your family or extended family who doesn't know Jesus? Commit fully to praying for this person, and reflect on whether God would have you do anything other than what you are currently doing.

3. Do you have a cycle-breaker in your extended family? If so, journal on the ways this person has changed your family.

4. Do you need to be a cycle-breaker for your family? If so, how?

11

Off Course

CIRCLE OF INTENTION: OUR JOB RELATIONSHIPS

PICTURE YOURSELF IN A sailing or motorized vessel out in the sometimes calm, oftentimes wild, ocean. I am not "Captain Nautical," so my experience with such things is not deep. One of my few endeavors in the actual ocean resulted in Lori and I going to a remote island of the San Juan Islands with another couple, Troy and Christy. We were using Troy's dad's boat, and in my circles, we did actually call Troy "Captain Nautical," as he had grown up around boats and always knew what to do with the boat whenever my buddies and I were out water skiing or wakeboarding. He always knew what to do with small boat repairs and the many details that come with getting the boat in and out of the water.

On this occasion, we had beached the boat on Sucia, a small island with no homes, but many walking paths created by people who had spent time on the island. We had an amazing day carrying a picnic onto our island hike, hiking sometimes right along the coastline, sometimes deeper into the forested land. It was a sunny, beautiful day and we had a great time connecting with our friends and the beautiful surroundings in which God had placed us. We regretfully called it a day and hiked back to the boat. When we rounded the corner, I could see Troy's surprised look as the color drained from his face.

Looking past Troy and down to the beach, I saw the Pharma-Sea, Troy's dad's boat sitting by itself on the beach. The boat was aptly named, as his dad was a pharmacist for many years. The Pharma-Sea was sitting in sand with the ocean about twenty to thirty yards behind it. The boat lay there slightly off to its side, sitting in sand and no water. Troy had misread the tide charts and mistakenly thought we had hours more before the tide went out in this narrow, shallow bay that we had entered. As he quickly reread the information he had, we realized we would be there for hours more on Sucia. We would have to wait for the tide to come back in before the Pharma-Sea would be in the water.

This has turned out to be a great memory and one that we have laughed at many a time. We ended up having a great day and one that I don't regret at all. I still remember sitting in the back of the Pharma-Sea as Troy steered it back to Bellingham on a day that now was on its last embers. The sun was setting behind us and Mount Baker was in front of us, in all of its snow-filled glory. I had my arm around the woman I loved, I was in God's creation, and I was with friends. Getting the boat beached turned out to be a blessing and a story that we share.

Sometimes in life we can have this similar experience in our following Jesus. I picture our faith as the Pharma-Sea, which carries us and which we rely on to get us where God wants us. Sometimes we climb out of the Pharma-Sea when we have a plan, and wander away to explore and live life, forgetting to check our facts and forgetting to check in on our relationship with God, making sure it is right and things are good. Before we know it, we are off wandering and not thinking about what got us to where we are and what we will rely on to get us home. We remember Jesus when we are done with our own agenda or when we are done "playing"; then we head back to God. God has promised he will be found when we seek him. However, when we wander back to God, sometimes we find that our lack of focus on him has the natural consequences of opportunities lost, costly detours, or missing the tide of what he meant to do through us or around us.

I had this experience a couple of years ago. We are called to excellence in our job—being skilled, working hard, seeking success as defined in our jobs. Being excellent is part of doing things to honor God. God did not call us to be lazy or unproductive or do things with a lack of passion. But I had a commitment to be about bigger things as well. I sought to influence my coaches and players by my faith and character. These were two of the biggest circles of intention I had. I sought to make it a journey about how I could use this platform to live for Jesus and have others be impacted positively. Lori, the kids, and I had spent several times during the autumn season, sitting in our empty gym, each of us sitting on the circle in the center of the gym and praying that this season would glorify Jesus.

Fast forward three months. I wearily pulled open the front door, had another 10:00 p.m. dinner/snack, and took care of the last few post-game day details that come with the territory. On this night, our season had ended as we lost the district playoffs convincingly in a game that was very disappointing to me, given how I felt we could have played better. It was one of many tough nights this year in which we had ended up on the lower end of the scoreboard more often than we preferred. Lori, as always, was up and waiting to hear me talk and I obliged, talking about the night, the year, and some of the frustrating situations that we as a team and coaches had dealt with. I trailed off with the words, "I thought we were going to have an amazing story, I thought we were going to come back, storm through the playoffs. I just thought it was going to be different."

My voice trailed off and as I looked at her face, I will forever be haunted by her tear-filled eyes and the words that followed. She looked at me with both love and sorrow, and a tear dripped off her chin. "I thought *you* were going to be different. I thought it wouldn't just be about the game this year." The words hung in the air and on my heart like a weight. My heart was cut to the core. My stomach immediately dropped.

Because she was right. "I thought *you* were going to be different."

I realized in that moment of time, that as much as I tried to make it about success both without and within, I had somehow forgotten to check on the "Pharma-Sea"; I had forgotten to read my "tide charts"; I had mistakenly followed the winding path that led me on my sole pursuit of winning and worldly success. As wins had become fewer and harder to come by, I had pursued them harder, more feverishly. This is okay, but not at the expense of the true mission of my season. I could now see Lori's heart. One that supports me, trusts that I am leading us in Jesus' name, one that prays for me to be about the things of Jesus, one that gives a lot up so I can pursue this time-consuming job. I could see that my lack of focus on Jesus 100 percent affected not only my chance to be a light to the guys and my coaches, but also to fulfill the purposes that bring joy and fulfillment to me and to Lori who shares this journey with me.

I was then, and even now, in a soul-searching place.

Am I capable of pursuing my job and doing it for Jesus completely?

Can I give Jesus my life and my job even when things aren't going as I plan?

Can I do my calling and not get caught up on the world's definition of success?

Am I holding Lori back and *us* back from something that God might want?

Why, after doing this for more than twenty-five years, do I still resort back to winning/losing/success only and *lose sight of* being a light, regardless of the ups and downs of life? "I thought you were going to be different." These words have got me thinking about what it would be like to one day ride the "Pharma-Sea" home after my last breath. I have been thinking about how sad it would be to hear Jesus say to me, "I thought you were going to be different." These words are so different than the "well done!" that I want my life to be about. Will I hear, "Well done, my good and faithful servant," or will I hear God's reflections on missed opportunities and his sorrow about how he thought "it wasn't going to be about worldly things"?

I wonder if you have been off course in trying to live out your faith at work and among the people with whom you share much of your life's hours interacting. I hope you are intentionally asking God how to use *your* workplace as *his working place*.

We all have different types of jobs and work with different types of people. Lori is in full-time ministry and spends much of her conversational and meeting time with other believers who are asking to be trained or for direction so that they can serve better. She deals with people who are seeking to partner with her and God in the ministry in which she is involved. Her outreach through her job is helping these fellow believers reach others who haven't yet experienced God and his grace. There are very distinct and unique challenges in working all day and every day with fellow believers.

I work in a public school and get to experience the wide swath of humanity that walks the halls every day. Those 1,850 kids that walk our hall, some of whom come in my classes and are on my teams, are looking for many different things; sometimes Jesus is the farthest thing from their minds. I swear I learn a new word from Urban Dictionary every day. I also work with people who I know love Jesus and many who outspokenly do not. The American public school really is a microcosm of society. Your workplace might be similar.

My dear friend Ryan and I have taught, figuratively, shoulder-to-shoulder for over fifteen years at the school. We have had countless hours of conversation leaning over our Buzz Inn Breakfast Specials, over our coffee tables in our homes, and even over the running trail, as Ryan runs easily and I gasp along, trying to make sure I ask lots of questions to save some breath. So many of our conversations have centered on, "How do I take my job in a very secular place, do it with great excellence, *and* make it every bit as much as I can about Jesus?" We have talked long and often about how to honor Jesus in a way that doesn't diminish or cost us our jobs or professional lives. Conversations have been raw, asking how we can do this job where we talk about Newton's laws of gravity, systems of equations, mitochondria, and the Pythagorean theorem and somehow glorify Jesus.

So, I write this chapter as one who is still searching and asking, trying to figure it all out. However, I do feel confident about the first place to begin in making your workplace part of your Mission My Town. To begin, we look closely at an Old Testament word with eternal relevance: *consecrate*. A Google search tell us that this word means to "Make or declare something sacred. Dedicate formally to a divine purpose." I love that! Let's take our jobs and make them sacred. Let's take our workplace and dedicate it formally to God's divine purpose.

One of the first mentions of the word *consecrate* in the Bible is when the Israelites were crossing from the dessert into the land for which they had been searching for forty years. Moses had died and our old friend Joshua had now been placed in leadership. Most people know by heart the story of God parting the Red Sea as the Israelites escaped from Egypt and Pharaoh's regime. It is a miraculous story of God's deliverance and most people know it well. For some reason, I never fully put it together that God used a similar experience to lead them from the desert into the promised land.

The Israelites had come to the Jordan and had camped out for three days when Joshua pulled them together and said, "Consecrate yourselves. For tomorrow the Lord will do amazing things among you" (Josh 3:5). And he did. The priests carried the ark of the covenant into the waters of the Jordan. One must understand that the Jordan would have been at flood stage this time of the year. The priests, who had consecrated themselves, stepped into the raging, swirling, full Jordan River, and then a miracle happened. The rushing waters stopped all the way upriver at another town called Adam as the priests reached the water's edge. The Israelites then began their new adventure the same way they had begun their escape: by doing the impossible and crossing on dry land.

Maybe it's time that you get set for a second stage of your career. Possibly, you need to consecrate yourself (and your job) because God is ready to do new and amazing things among you and through you. Maybe you are shaking your head and saying, "Mark, you don't understand. I work in a very secular or even anti-God workplace." So did Moses when God called him into the Mission My Town of leading the Israelites. It required Moses to have a repurposing of his life and the tools of his life.

Moses came before Pharaoh begrudgingly, having already tried to talk his way out of serving God in this role. However, here he stood, in front of one of the most feared leaders in the world, about to bargain for the Israelites' release. God told Moses, "Take your staff and throw it down before Pharaoh and it will become a snake" (Exod 7:9). I am struck by the symbolism for Moses at this moment.

You see, Moses had spent the last forty years of his life using this staff for his job. This was his shepherd's staff, which he had used skillfully in his job taking care of sheep. God was asking to repurpose Moses' tools to do miraculous things for him. Possibly, he is asking you and me to do the same. You are not too old, too young, too far into your career, or not far enough. No excuses. We learn right before this, that the Moses standing before Pharaoh about to throw down his staff was eighty-three years old. He wasn't too old for God to repurpose his life and calling.

Peter also was asked to do the same. Jesus knew he was a passionate, skilled, experienced fisherman. So, I can imagine the sly smile Peter may have shown when Jesus asked him to throw his nets over the other side of the boat. You see, Peter had fished these waters for years. He had also fished all night and not caught a fish. So, there had to be a slight bit of eye-rolling when he tossed his nets out. And then Peter's world was rocked as the boat couldn't even contain the fish being caught. Jesus was using Peter's calling to speak to him. And later he used his job as a symbol of his new calling. "I will make you fishers of men" (Matt 4:19). Peter thought his whole life had been geared towards catching fish. Jesus gave him a mission so much greater.

So, how do I repurpose my gavel, shovel, tractor, lesson plans, clipboard, ball, tax reports, staff meetings, laptop, or sales quotas for God?

That is up to you and God. I believe if you consecrate your job or career to him, allow him to repurpose the tools of your trade and the methods of your business, he will begin to show you specifically how he wants to use the uniquely created *you* in the most powerful way.

My teacher friend Ryan carries a clipboard for each of his classes with all the students' names on it. Rather than putting assignment scores or attendance, he puts an "P" for each kid he prays for and a "C" for each kid he has a conversation with every day.

My coaching friend Bary asks for the Holy Spirit to direct him every time he gives a pre-game talk or halftime speech. He is unashamed to tell his players that he loves them and to walk alongside them when they make some tough choices.

My close friend Matt is a soccer coach and AP teacher. He combines high expectations in class and on the field with love and character development. He shows Jesus to his players and students without ever talking about him.

My friends Scott and Christa use their successful local business to serve Jesus also. They look for countless ways to use the financial success of their business to impact local ministries.

A local high school soccer coach, Matt, uses his love for soccer and Jesus in leading Adventure Soccer. Matt and his family serve orphans in Swaziland by providing not only soccer clinics, but food and care as well.

In his book *All In*, Mark Batterson relates the story of Johann Sebastian Bach. We all have probably heard of this great composer. We have all certainly sat through a hot summer wedding where the bride came down the aisle to his famous bridal march. Bach had over one thousand known compositions. What I didn't know is that in the margin of each original composition, he wrote the letters SDG, which stood for the Latin phrase *Soli Deo Gloria*. This phrase means "to the glory of God alone." What is the margin of your work where you can do SDG?

As Batterson goes on to say:

"It's not about what you do.

It's about why you do what you do.

Ultimately, it is about who you do it for."[1]

JOURNAL AND REFLECTION QUESTIONS:

1. Have you ever considered your job as your ministry?

1. Batterson, *All In*, 118.

2. What are the "tools of the trade" that you could repurpose for his purpose? Specifically, how would it look different for you than it has up to now?

3. Do you have any partners at your workplace who you could ask to join you in your Mission My Town at your job?

4. Journal about what it might look like if Jesus came into your workplace, took your exact job, and did it in place of you.

12

Play Time

CIRCLE OF INTENTION: RECREATIONAL PURSUITS

Do you remember our family motto from earlier: "We love God, we serve others, we work hard, we *play* hard"? I am a firm believer that God desires us to find enjoyment and recreation in life. I believe he placed some unique things in our hearts that we were hard-wired to enjoy. Pursuing these passions in the proper balance is something that can deepen our walk with God as we experience joy in the pleasure of these things. Finding space for recreating is life-giving. God has given us an incredible gift in allowing us the special thrill or relaxation or fulfillment that these areas of our lives bring. At the same time, it is also a way for you to bring glory back to the great Creator who made these things to hold so much special joy. In this Mission My Town, even these are areas that can bring others toward God if we are mindful.

So, what makes you come alive? What do you look forward to doing when the demands of work, family, and schedule end and your play starts? For some, it is the thrill of blasting down the mountain on skis or a snowboard in fresh powder and blue skies. Others might enjoy the quiet, systematic process of quilting. Many people find their expression or release in music or art. Some have hobbies, such as collectibles or scrapbooking. It might be the challenge and release that accompanies running or lifting or fitness competitions. You might enjoy video games, puzzles, or the Rubik's

Cube. If you are like me, you love the competition and fitness of basketball or tennis.

Did you even think that these might not only be gifts for you to enjoy, but also to bring you *and* others closer to Jesus in a unique manner?

I think of the many ways I have seen God work through a simple tennis match with a buddy. After a grueling three-set match, in which we exchanged shot after shot, competed to the best of our abilities, and laughed and groaned in frustration, often the best part of these matches happened while sitting on the ground, sipping Gatorade, covered in sweat. After initially laughing about some of the funny points or shaking our heads in frustration over shots missed or opportunities lost, often some of the best conversations I have had have surfaced. "How is it going with your wife?" "Any success with parenting lately?" "How did that tough situation go with your co-worker that you were telling me about?" Some of these moments have been connecting conversations that often ended in prayer for another follower of Jesus. Some of these conversations have been my first window to talk about my faith and what Jesus is doing with me or has done in my life.

Of course, every one of my good friends who have played against me in basketball will be smirking and giving each other a knowing smile right now. Because sometimes, my recreational pursuits have not honored God. I believe that God has given me a very strong competitive nature. I wouldn't be able to do the job I have in coaching without the unique wiring that allows me to love to compete. But, as with all gifts, it is to be exercised in a way that God intended. I am ashamed to admit how many biting comments I have delivered in the heat of the battle. Maybe it was a foul on game point that didn't have to be so physical. Sometimes I have acted in a way that was flat out embarrassing, all in the name of "competitiveness." So, this is one of those areas in which I have fallen short at times. That being said, my time in gyms over the past decades has brought many great friendships, conversations, and ministry opportunities.

In particular with sports, I think back to a clarifying moment recently with one of my friends, Jeff. Jeff is a guy who didn't start playing much basketball until after high school and college. He came to the game late and missed many of the fundamentals people who have been immersed in the game have. But he absolutely loves playing, makes time to play a couple times a week, and is a sponge when it comes to learning what he can about the fundamentals, patterns, and intricacies of the game. I love playing with Jeff because he plays hard, is a great teammate, and gets after it.

Something happened a few weeks ago in a game that caught me so off guard, mainly because my response would have been so much different than Jeff's. Although we love to be on the same team, this particular day, we were not much of the time. I was having a good day, as were some of my teammates, and Jeff's team was struggling to get wins. The final game of the day was different. Our teams went back and forth the entire game, never separated by more than a point. We were playing "win by two" to 21 points. The game was so fun and competitive, and nobody was able to seal the deal. Jeff and I were guarding each other throughout the game. The score was 27 to 27, when I came off a screen, let a shot fly, and heard a swish. The next thing I knew, someone was hugging me from the side. I looked over and Jeff had a smile a mile wide and was saying, "Awesome shot, man. I had a hand in your face and everything." He was truly excited for me, one of his best friends. The moment was especially convicting as I realized that, had the shoe been on the other proverbial foot, I would have reluctantly shaken his hand, all the while, kicking myself for getting caught on a screen and giving up a game winner. It made me realize that recreational pursuits can be serious, but there is a much bigger reason why we play.

Think about the Circle of Intention of your hobbies and recreational pursuits. Seriously, really look back at what you wrote down in the Circles of Intention chapter. Who are the people you see and experience these activities with?

Do the women at your yoga class see your participation and interactions differently because you know Jesus? When you and your buddies get together for cigars and poker, do you engage and enjoy and still bring honor to God? Do your rock-climbing buddies know you to be a confident, capable encourager or a skilled know-it-all that shows more pride than confident humility? When your wine or book club gets together, does gossip run through you? When you lose yourself in video games, do you do so in a way that gives you a healthy release or does your family lose out?

In pursuit of play and recreation, sometimes Jesus' example is not helpful. Matthew, Mark, Luke, and John don't give us any great insight into whether Jesus played bocce ball with the guys or threw a camel skin frisbee around the disc course of Jerusalem. I would like to think he threw on the Air Jerusalems and played some mean pick-up basketball, but I guess the game wasn't around yet, sadly. I guess He recreated by raising people from the dead and other assorted miracles.

However, I do know that the Bible asks us to have a rhythm of work and release. Even back as early as the creation of the world, God himself gave us the example of working hard then resting. I figure if the God of the universe needs rest or at least models rest, I probably should as well. In the second book of the Bible, God clearly commands his people: "Remember the Sabbath day by keeping it holy. Six days you shall labor and do all your work, but the seventh day is a Sabbath to the Lord your God" (Exod 2:8–10).

So, possibly this is a chapter you scoff at and say, "I have no time to relax or to pursue any recreational pursuits." I can certainly relate as I spent much of my life that way. However, what looks restricting is actually one of God's greatest gifts to us in terms of a Sabbath or rest. He created us. He knows us in general as people and he knows you and me specifically as his children. He knows how we are wired, our needs, desires, loves, and passions. He gives us a command to take some time each week to take a break. If we flip the script and look at the Sabbath as one of his great gifts, I promise you won't be disappointed.

Lori and I were caught up in a whirlwind lifestyle and pace for many years. One day I realized that keeping the Sabbath was just as much one of his commands and desires as not committing adultery and honoring our fathers and mothers. I was being disobedient by trying to use more days of the week, in many ways to honor him, through ministry. Sabbath is not an excuse for ditching your family and pursuing your own hobbies at the expense of your family. However, in our taking a break on a weekly basis, we do want to find ways to replenish our souls and hearts.

My wife is way more unselfish than I am. She struggles to be an advocate for herself when she is balancing the whole life, wife, kids, job pace of life. One time I tried to get her to understand what I call the "flight attendant motto." Anyone who has ever flown has tuned out these wonderful people as they politely talk about safety procedures. One time I was particularly struck by the phrase: "Make sure to put on your oxygen mask before helping others." I thought about the selfishness of doing this if ever potentially in the situation where my kids need help. The truth is I wouldn't be able to help my kids if I didn't take the small amount of time to put my own mask on, and then help them. I would pass out and potentially not be able to help them either. I believe that there is a great wisdom in this phrase, if not taken to the extreme. We are better able to serve the needs of others if we take some time to make sure we are getting energized. We can't be our best self for others' benefit without taking some time to be re-energized spiritually, emotionally, and physically.

If you have recreational pursuits, I challenge you to fully consider how you could best participate in these in a way that further your Mission My Town approach to your faith and disciple-making. If you don't have any recreational pursuits, I challenge you to look at your life and schedule and try to find *some* time to carve out. This isn't a ticket to abuse and misuse time spent recreating, but I would challenge you that you can't be your best self without some type of downtime. God made us to have some built-in breaks.

JOURNAL AND REFLECTION QUESTIONS:

1. What is it that you love to do in your spare time? What brings you joy and release from life's pressures and activity?

2. Are there other people involved in these pursuits? How have you done using these activities to witness to them?

3. Do you take a sabbath? If so, what does it look like? If not, how are you going to adjust your life and schedule to honor God in this area of your life?

4. What are your biggest struggles to glorify God in these recreational pursuits?

13

Soccer Mom, Coach Dad

CIRCLE OF INTENTION: BASIC LIFE INTERACTIONS

LET'S FACE IT; IT rains a lot in the Pacific Northwest. A lot. It keeps everything beautiful, but there are long stretches where even someone with the most optimistic, positive mindset gets tired of umbrellas, muddy pant legs, wet work documents, choosing a movie rather than a hike, and so on. It was one of these long, wet autumn days that God used to get my attention.

As I watched my son playing soccer on the soaked field, I looked around the sidelines. Max's team had played nearly an entire season's worth of games at this point. As my gaze scanned our sideline, I observed one shade after another. As a side note, the term "shade" really is not an apt descriptor of the purpose it serves in Washington. It is actually a glorified eight-by-eight-foot umbrella with legs on it. These collapsible shelters were lined up and down our sideline. As I scanned the faces underneath these, God caught my attention in a way that only he can.

I suddenly realized I had gone almost an entire soccer season without really getting to know any of these people better. I hadn't invested any energy at all to "earn the right to be heard." This is a term we use in Young Life ministry that fits Jesus' ministry model perfectly. Through relationships and living in a way that is contagious and different, one would hope to have the right to show Jesus or even talk about Jesus. I suddenly realized I would go to Max's practice and do work, get on my phone, or even retreat to my car to do these things. During games, I hadn't taken the initiative to get out from underneath my soccer shade, or for that matter, my comfort level, to get to know anyone.

I felt like Ronald Wayne. You are probably asking who is Ronald Wayne? Great question; common question. But first let me remind you of two other people that you have probably heard of. Steve Jobs was the CEO and co-founder of Apple. If you have seen the movie of his life, he is a fascinating, talented man who made the most of every opportunity seemingly. He was also CEO and majority owner of Pixar and on the board of directors for Walt Disney Company. He is considered a visionary in the computing industry. You may have also heard of Steve Wozniak. In conjunction with Jobs, he is one of the co-founders of Apple and almost single-handedly developed the Apple 1 and 2 computers, which are credited for beginning the personal computing revolution of the seventies and eighties. Early on, in the infancy of their partnership, Jobs convinced Wozniak that they needed to own their own company. They sold some of their most valuable possessions, including Wozniak's graphing calculator and Job's Volkswagen Van to net $1,300 and start their business out of Job's bedroom and later out of his garage as they ran out of space.

On April 1, 1976 they formed the Apple computer, along with Ronald Wayne. Wayne was the administrative supervisor and 10 percent owner. Wayne developed the first logo, wrote the original business partnership, and wrote the manual for the Apple 1. Less than two weeks into the partnership, Wayne relinquished his portion for $800. He also accepted $1,500 to forfeit any future claims against Apple. We all know the enormous success of Apple over time. Had Wayne kept his 10 percent share of Apple, it would have been worth $75.5 *billion* as of March 2017.[1] What a missed opportunity financially.

I don't want to be the Ronald Wayne of Mission My Town. Not financially, but in terms of kingdom investment. I want to be able to have wisdom and discernment when I have an opportunity with this (and all) Circles of Intention. Sometimes I wonder if I miss God's working around me and through me in my daily interactions with people. I wonder if I was more attuned to the Holy Spirit and more engaged in the present, if I might have more chance to impact people I interact with daily, or at least often. I don't want to miss a $75.5 billion spiritual investment into the lives of

---

1. Wikipedia, "Steve Jobs"; Wikipedia, "Ronald Wayne"; Wikipedia, "Steve Wozniak."

people because I might be preoccupied with my own $800 investment into my own problems or insecurities.

My friend Jeff is the Steve Jobs of investing in the daily, common interactions. He is a regional director for Young Life and is a very gifted, relational person. My friends and I always joke that Jeff has "a guy" for whatever situation. Car problems? No worries, Jeff knows a guy. Need to rent a limo? Jeff knows a guy (literally). Need to cement a driveway? Jeff knows a guy. He not only knows the guy, the guy comes within one day and cements Jeff's driveway because of Jeff's winsome ways. Need an Airbnb? Jeff knows a guy (family). Jeff has all these "guys" and "girls" because he takes every interaction as important. He wins barbers over, receptionists over, and so on because he is engaging and caring on the surface; in reality, that surface is a reflection of his heart for their hearts.

I wonder how many of these daily situations we miss to invest in those people we naturally see often and regularly. I wonder if you have any carpools, practices, yoga groups, CrossFit groups, and so on that might become of your Circles of Intention. If you are a parent, it seems like so many of the people we interact often with are a result of the activities our kids are involved in. Maybe you see the same parents or grandparents at drama practice, dance recitals, band performances, the dojo, or sports practices and games. We mostly experience polite smiles and welcomes, small talk, and then everyone goes to their proverbial corner. Be different; take a risk; start a conversation. Allow this to be a circle in which God uses you over time.

There are many basic life functions most of us do. We go to the grocery store, buy gas, do the drive-thru at the coffee stand, go to the post office, get our oil changed, get haircuts, take the dog to the groomer, and so on. What do your interactions look like with the people you interact with at these places? Are you polite, yet guarded? Are you impatient while waiting for the latte that took forty-five extra seconds to make? Or do you take notice when a barista seems to be having a tough day? Do you show kindness to the new checker who seems to always produce the longest wait? Deeper still, do you pray for and look for windows of meaningful conversations with these people you see often?

Jesus made the most of these opportunities.

He engaged with the woman at the well and learned her story. This interaction came about due to the basic and daily task of getting water. In Matthew 9, the Bible tells us when he came to his own town, some men brought him a paralytic. Jesus then went on to heal him and minister to his heart after simply encountering him walking through "his own town." A Sabbath walk through a grain field with his friends and disciples resulted in a teachable moment about grace versus law. Another time he was at a friends' house having dinner, just doing life. Some Pharisees saw that Jesus was eating with "sinners," this basic life interaction turned into a beautiful description of how Jesus came to save the lost; the people who really needed him. Jesus could recognize when a divine opportunity developed out of a very ordinary situation. Let's pray to be able to do the same.

Are you winsome or are you whine-some? Are you engaging or are you dismissive? Are you someone who brings joy, kindness, or fun to their day or are you another forgettable person? Are you Jesus to them in some small way? Let's look to use every day as a holy day for Jesus to do something through us. All that it really takes is being attuned to the Holy Spirit and what he would have us do or say, or not say or not do.

JOURNAL AND REFLECTION QUESTIONS:

1. List some of the people you interact with on a regular or somewhat regular basis just "doing life." Next to each one, score yourself on a 1–10 scale of intentionality of building relationship.

2. Who are some of these people that you sense God might be leading you to be more engaged with? Is there someone in this Circle of Intention that you may have already earned the right to enter into some type of spiritual conversation?

3. Do you have anyone who has impacted you in this manner?

4. Who is someone that right now just needs to see a kind face or joyful disposition that you could bring on a consistent basis?

14

Shishkabats and the Village

DO YOU EVER TAKE time to reflect on your history with your closest brothers and sisters in Christ? I think it is fun and even healthy every once in a while to reflect on how God brought you together with your spouse or your friends who walk closely with you through life. It is fun to see how God knits lives together.

I think back to an awkward time thirteen years ago. We had been invited by our friends Jeff and Tanya to the home of someone we didn't know. As we searched in the dark for the right house on Lake Drive, we finally found it and walked toward the front door. We didn't know a lot of things about this night. First of all, we didn't know anyone besides Jeff and Tanya. Secondly, we really didn't know why we were getting together. (My cynical side pictured a pyramid marketing scheme presentation.) Thirdly, we had no idea how this awkward night would end up impacting our lives between then and now.

Jeff had loosely described this as a group that got together, ate dinner together, and talked about God and marriage. We settled in, introduced ourselves, then tried just to learn names, let alone the stories of these people's lives. As leaders and Type A personalities, we both got back in the car at the end of the night, questioning what kind of goals the group had, what was the organization of the night, and was this the best use of our relational time. Despite our cynicism, we trusted Jeff and Tanya, liked the new couples we had met, and felt God's call to invest in this group.

This group of people began to be called our "small group." I know that in the current culture of small groups, our small group does not meet the usual church-directed mandates of the structure of "small groups." We were not part of the same church. We were not called to get together and talk about the sermon from last week or pad the family-ministry numbers. We were not being called to be together for a year, then to divide and multiply into other small groups.

In short, we were a group of people that were committed to doing life together.

Over the past fifteen years, this group has grown, shrunk, changed direction, mourned, celebrated, called each other out, had each other's backs, and participated in the biggest, most significant parts of each other's lives. We have seen one of our couples divorce. We have seen families have children and adopt children. We have watched each other struggle with the loss of parents. Physical pain, surgeries, premarital pregnancy, house repossession, questioning God, wayward children, baptizing kids, new jobs and ministries, group dates, and vacations all have been part of this story of our small group. Of the original couples, only ourselves, Jeff and Tanya, and Troy and Christy remain. Other families have come and gone as life has changed. But three other families have joined seamlessly and we have enriched one another's lives.

I think about Jeff. When we first met, Lori and I were serving for four weeks at a Young Life camp. Jeff and Tanya were serving at the same camp. I thought Jeff was hilarious—and a loose cannon. I saw greatness and leader-ship in him. I also sometimes saw immaturity and people-pleasing. Now I see him as a godly leader of men and mentor to many. He speaks into my life in the deepest of ways.

I think about how I met Ryan. We both were new teachers and the district decided to strike. So, here I was: I knew nobody and was walking the streets with a bunch of others holding picket signs. I noticed another guy who seemed to be looking around, and I approached him. My friend-ship with Ryan has grown from strangers awkwardly holding picket signs together to meeting every week for breakfast and going as deep as two guys can.

I think about Kyle. The first time I met Kyle, I was taken aback at his frankness and directness. What first startled me about him is now what I most appreciate. Kyle is a straight shooter who will look you in the eye and tell you the truth in love. Kyle also uses his home and all his resources to the betterment of the kingdom. I have learned so much about what it means to use your "stuff" for Jesus.

I think about Marcus, a man I coached and mentored when he was in high school and is now part of our small group. Marcus would not only give you the shirt off his back, he would give you his pants and shoes as well. Whether it be 2:00 a.m. or in the middle of the day, he will come to your aid in a pinch. He is a committed and faithful friend who also happens to have the gift of humor and storytelling like no other.

I think about Troy. In our time together in our small group, I have seen him grow from a tentative family leader to one who leads with confidence and love. He is a man who shows me what it looks like to be an engaged, selfless father to his kids as well. From Troy I have learned what it means to use God's financial provision with wisdom. Troy and I have connected over tennis, hoops, and running. He is fun and faithful.

We were called to move to Lake Stevens, while Jeff and Tanya were in Everett. When they heard we were moving, they were so excited. They connected us with people, shared input on the area, and (this will date our relationship) Jeff even made me a worship *cassette tape* to listen to as I drove back and forth that summer between our old home and our new home. Then the fateful night happened that I described earlier, and our lives are forever deeply intertwined.

This immature guy has become a respected and wise leader without losing his sense of humor and fun. This guy whose depth I questioned has been part of some of the deepest conversations I have had with someone other than my wife. Jeff, Ryan, Troy, Marcus, and Kyle know me as well as anyone. They know my victories and struggles. I would suggest that if you don't have these types of relationships in your life, you are really missing out on what God intends for his followers.

We all have long been part of the same fantasy football league as well. Not to brag, but I may or may not have just finished second in the league this year. One rule of our league is that teams need to be named after locations and then a "thing" that makes a play on words. Hours have been spent coming up with team names. Some of these names are not appropriate for writing here. Others include: The Palouse Bowels; Coulee Dam Politicians; Laos Lobos; Melbourne Ultimatums; Tijuana Bees; Ludlow Riders; Lacey Underwear; Helena Handbasket; the list goes on.

One night at our small group, the guys had decided we were going to try to be more consistent touching base throughout the week and sharing. We created a private Facebook group and were deciding on the name. An hour of laughter and names followed, very similar to our fantasy football names. Eventually, and I don't know how, we settled on "The Shishkabats." There is no rhyme or reason, but that is the name of our site where we have shared life—our struggles, joys, failures, and triumphs. It has loosely become our guys' small group "mascot." Similarly, but with much more maturity, the ladies of the group came up with a name that symbolizes their bond: "The Village." Have you heard the phrase, "it takes a village to raise a child"? Well, our small group has this feature and beyond. We truly are endeavoring to do real life together. We are looking to lift each other up in our marriages, parenting, and relationship with Jesus.

The following story describes our small group. Lori had a medical emergency that was scary and sudden. I found myself following an ambulance, my two-year-old daughter with me, my wife in the ambulance ahead, and not knowing what I would do. I called a small group member. The next thing I received was a text describing how our daughter would be taken care of by a rotation of three families while I attended to what Lori needed. Our desperate hour involved a surgery at 2:00 a.m., prayerful hours spent at Lori's side, and also peace knowing my daughter was being loved and cared for by the closest non-family members I knew.

Likewise, I have had the great blessing of having accountability and support that I think few people get to experience. I have had small group guys lovingly and supportively call me out on how I was parenting. I have sat down across a Starbucks table and challenged another man in our small group to rise up and support his wife in a way that showed her more love. For fifteen years, a couple of times a month, I have been able to look around a circle of guys with whom I could laugh, pray, be real, and really experience life. It really has been a life-changing experience to realize that there is more to life than what most men experience; there is vulnerability steeped in deep trust that has been earned over time; there is deep laughter that can be followed by deep discourse on what God is doing in our lives—or how we are hindering what God is trying to do.

I have spent the past several pages talking about me and what I have gotten to experience in the form of our small group. I feel that I have been extremely blessed to have a group of like-minded people who have committed to each other for such a length of time. However, what this has really taught me is that this is "the church" that Jesus established in the Bible. This experience has taught me that I want others to experience this as well. I want *you* to experience this form of relationship that is a small piece of heaven on earth.

If you have never read Acts, you need to do so. It is an amazing re-telling of how the disciples and early church members impacted their region in a huge way for Jesus. It is so cool to see the Holy Spirit work miracles time and time again in and through these early church leaders. But a bigger miracle might be what we find in Acts 4:

> All the believers were one in heart and mind. No one claimed that any of their possessions was their own, but they shared everything they had. With great power the apostles continued to testify to the resurrection of the Lord Jesus. And God's grace was so powerfully at work in them all that there were no needy persons among them. For from time to time those who owned land or houses sold them, brought the money from the sales and put it at the apostles' feet, and it was distributed to anyone who had need.

To me, this is a miracle: to see people put others' needs above their own; to see people hold what they have loosely; to see people lost in the mission of Jesus so much that they don't count the cost. While your small group members might not sell their house and give you the proceeds, I do pray that you can experience this type of "being one in heart and mind," and this level of sharing life, even resources when necessary.

"Good for you, Mark; I have no group of people in my life and I couldn't even think of where to begin." Maybe you just moved and enrolled at a college far from home. Possibly you have been too busy with school, work, and family that you haven't had time to explore getting involved on a deeper level with someone. You may have even lived where you are for years and years and struggled to have this type of group present itself. The truth of the matter is that these things don't always just show up; sometimes you need to put in some relational investment.

There are many ways for these types of deep connections to grow with another person or a group of people. Ours has grown organically, with reliance on God, when we bring a new family into the group that needs what we have to offer. I have seen small groups work very effectively at a church where strangers are put together. God can make any situation work, but you have to start. Inertia is a real thing in the human condition: if we are moving, we will stay moving. If we are at rest, we will continue to stay at rest in terms of finding relational and spiritual connection.

If you really can't think of someone or a group of people that you can see yourself going deep with, I would suggest a start. Think about your whole community and your circles we have been talking about. Is there another person who could either be your mentor or seems to have a similar interest in growing in Christ? Have coffee or breakfast with them and share your heart to meet and go deep. Maybe you decide on reading a book of the Bible together or doing a study, or reading a Christian classic together.

Look at the life of Jesus. He ministered to the whole "community," or region, around him. He cared for the needs of strangers. He also lived a majority of his documented life in a group. His twelve disciples were his group of people with whom he laughed, served, challenged, discoursed, and served. However, Jesus took it one step further: he had an inner circle. His group of Peter, James, and John were the guys he let into his life the most, seemingly. They, and no others, got to see him raise Jairus' daughter from the dead. He chose them to go to the mountaintop to see him be transfigured. Even on the night before his death, he asked them specifically to come further and pray with him.

So to recap and apply to our lives: he served his community; he did life and ministry in a group with others; he deeply invested in a small group of three guys; and he did it all in the name of his Father. If you have these things present in your life, be thankful and rejoice. If you don't, let's not let inertia get the best of you. Pray for direction and people to partner with; actively think and look for the right fit for you to do deep life with. The reward is well worth it.

JOURNAL AND REFLECTION QUESTIONS:

1. Do you have a close group of Christian brothers or sisters? Who would fit this description the most closely?

2. If this is absent from your life, what have you tried that has been successful/unsuccessful in the past?

3. If you don't have a "small group" of other disciples of Jesus, how are you getting accountability, encouragement, and support as you walk in your faith?

4. If you have a small group, is there someone else God might be prompting you to add to your group who could really benefit from what you have?

15

Time, Talent, Treasure

CIRCLE OF INTENTION: YOUR MINISTRY

WHAT ARE YOUR MAIN ministries? Where do you put your treasure, time, or talent? All three of these t's are important components of every ministry. Lori and I have found that we have fluctuated on which of these we were using most based on our life circumstances. For example, as newlyweds with no kids, we poured much of our resources and talent into giving our time. Once we had two young, needy kids in the house, our lives looked different and we had a season of life where our treasure was more of what we could give. However, I do want you to consider which components of your ministry really makes you excited. Also, which of your ministries has God really wired you to do?

It has been said that you can best judge someone's true priorities by looking at their bank account and their schedule app on their phone. How and where we spend our time and money really is the measuring stick of what we hold dear. God wants us to be good stewards of our time, treasure, and talent.

The Bible is famously misquoted in many ways. One I hear people say is, "Money is the root of all evil." Jesus never said that, and neither does the rest of the Bible. Instead it says (italics mine): "For the *love* of money is *a root of all kinds* of evil. Some people, eager for money, have wandered from the faith and pierced themselves with many griefs" (1 Tim 6:10). Jesus never said money itself was a bad thing. However, he did say, "Again I tell you, it is easier for a camel to go through the eye of a needle than for someone who is rich to enter the kingdom of God" (Matt 19:24). I believe that Jesus was talking about the challenge in being rich in *anything*: money, looks, athletic talent, people skills, and so on. It is when we make these things our kingdom that they get in our way.

Money is mentioned more than eight hundred times in the Bible.[1] More than prayer, healing, or mercy. The way we spend, save, utilize, lend, and steward our money seems to be very important to God. I believe for many people, money is the hardest area of their life to trust completely to God. In the story of the rich young ruler, his wealth was not the issue; the issue was that his wealth was more lord of his life than the Lord. However, it is possible for money to be one of our greatest ministry tools as well.

The Bible is full of rich people. Abraham was rich in cattle, silver, and gold. Isaac had flocks, possessions, and great herds of animals. David and his son Solomon were some of the richest men who ever lived. Hezekiah had storehouses of silver, gold, and jewels. Even the man that came and asked Pilate for Jesus' body, Joseph, was very wealthy.

One of the most beautiful and powerful expressions I get to see is how people use their wealth to bless others. In our jobs in teaching and ministry, Lori and I have been blessed time and time again by people who have lots of "stuff." People have allowed us to use two-million-dollar homes to host ministry events and retreats. People have allowed us to use $50,000 boats to pull kids in tubes and wakeboards at camp. People have let us use their $40,000 car while they are out of town. Someone even blessed us by letting us live in his house on the lake for a year so we could use it for God's purposes. I know many people who desire wealth because they know they are good at using their treasure for God's purposes.

An influential person I met in college at Pacific Lutheran University was a local businessman who mentored my roommates. He had a very successful business, so I was a bit surprised to go to his house one time and find he lived in a fairly simple home. Later that night, I asked my roommate about it and what he said still reverberates in my mind and challenges me to this day. This businessman and his wife had decided to figure out how much they truly needed to live, to care for their kids, and to prepare for future events, such as college costs. They vowed to live on this much wealth every year and give the rest to kingdom causes.

1. Nance-Nash, "Is the Bible?," line 6.

Another person who forever rocked my world was a volunteer tennis coach; we will call him "Joe" even though we won't learn his true name. Joe coached with someone we will call "Drew." Joe gave his time to help coach the tennis team for no pay at all. He also taught at the local high school. He would daily come to school in simple polo shirts and khaki pants. He drove a car with over 150,000 miles on it. Drew knew that finances were probably difficult for Joe, so behind his back, this head coach went to bat for Joe to get him a partial stipend. After a few meetings and quite a bit of time, Drew was happy to approach Joe and let him know they would be able to pay him some money. Joe smiled humbly, and said, "You really shouldn't have. But thank you." Drew had become convicted because Joe would often buy him treats and coffee, and was actually losing money in time, fuel, and drinks helping him coach his team.

After a couple years working together, Drew was called to take a new teaching job elsewhere. Joe came one day and pulled Drew aside and said they needed to talk. He proceeded to share with Drew that the place Drew was moving was someplace he had previously lived. This was not a surprise to as they had talked about it before. However, Joe said, "So, I want you to hear this from me, rather than somebody there. Hardly anybody knows what I am about to tell you, but just in case, I want to be the one to tell you. The truth is, I won the lottery a few years ago." Drew's mind replayed all that he knew about Joe: simple polos and khakis, the beat-up car, getting him a stipend, and so on. Joe continued to say that he didn't need to teach, but knew it was his way to give to the world and for his kids to see the value of hard work and purpose. His own kids didn't even know he had won the lottery. He talked about how he and his wife knew that this was a blessing given to them to bless others. They supported missionaries and causes all over the world. This true story of Joe's character and use of his wealth changed my view on stewardship, after Drew received permission to share it with me for this book.

The truth is, if you are reading this book, you are probably rich compared to most of the world. What? The average American income is $105 per day.[2] At the same time, there are over a billion people in less developed countries who live in extreme poverty, living on less than one dollar per day. It is staggering to think that even people with "modest" means in the United States can influence the basic needs of the poorest of the poor.

2. Stearns, *Hole in Gospel Summary*, 3.

One of the most impactful books I have read in the past few years is Richard Stearns' *The Hole in Our Gospel*. Richard was able to spend time with former president Jimmy Carter and shared part of Carter's speech for his Nobel Peace Prize:

> "At the beginning of this new millennium I was asked to discuss the greatest challenge that the world faces. Among all the possible choices, I decided that the most serious and universal problem is the growing chasm between the richest and poorest people on earth. Citizens of the ten wealthiest countries are now seventy-five times richer than those who live in the ten poorest ones, and the separation is increasing every year, not only between nations but also within them. The results of this disparity are the root causes of most of the world's unresolved problems, including starvation, illiteracy, environmental degradation, violent conflicts, and unnecessary illnesses that range from Guinea worms to HIV/AIDS."[3]

Stearns then goes on to show that the "hole" in the gospel for most of us is truly taking the commands of Jesus to heart about loving our neighbors, taking care of the poor and hungry, and seeking justice.[4] Hosea 6:6 says, "For I desire mercy, not sacrifice, and acknowledgement of God rather than burnt offerings."

After reading Stearns' book, I did something that he mentioned: I found every verse in the Bible mentioning poverty, wealth, justice, and oppression. I then had my teacher's assistants go through and cut out every one of these verses from all sixty-six books of the Bible. The result was a tattered book that looked like it was going to fall apart. My tattered Bible was the reminder of how much of the gospel we are ignoring if we don't take God's words seriously.

So, you and I are truly richer than we realize. The real question is how will we use that wealth?

"The true gospel is a call to self-denial, not self-fulfillment," John MacArthur.[5]

"In the end, we will remember not the words of our enemies, but the silence of our friends," Dr. Martin Luther King.[6]

---

3. Stearns, *Hole in Gospel*, 98.

4. Stearns, *Hole in Gospel Summary*, 1.

5. Goodreads, "MacArthur Quotes," quote 4, https://www.goodreads.com/author/quotes/1058367.John_F_MacArthur_Jr_.

6. Brainy Quote, "Martin Luther King Quotes," quote 1, https://www.brainyquote.com/authors/martin_luther_king_jr.

"But if anyone has material possessions and sees a brother or sister in need but has no pity on them, how can the love of God be in that person?" (1 John 3:17).

Are you using your treasure in your town for God's purposes? Is he prompting your heart right now with a need that you could meet someplace in your community or further across the globe—whether it be hunger, poverty, or use of dollars to promote ministries? Let the words above from Dr. King ever haunt us. Use your treasure as God prompts you. Your ministry might be a giving ministry.

We talked about the disparity in the world's income. There is one resource that is equitable to everyone in the world. Time: twenty-four hours; 1,440 minutes; 86,400 seconds. We all have the same exact gift every day. The way we use our time speaks volumes about us.

In your Mission My Town, is there a cause or need that God may have been calling you toward? You may be thinking several thoughts. I live on a fixed income. I live on a college student's lack of income. I am not a great public speaker. I don't have any obvious talents to use for the kingdom. We will talk about talents soon; what we all have is the ability to give time. The truth is that time is your most valuable and precious gift you can give away. Unlike money, which can always be re-earned, you cannot get time back that you give away.

In my experience, if you ask anyone, the vast majority will tell you they are busy. The truth is that most of us have more discretionary time than we realize. In an American Time Use Survey in 2016, the average person fifteen years and older spent almos five hours of their day on leisure activities, with 2.7 hours of this being watching TV.[7] I can't even imagine how much time most of us spend on activities related to our cell phone. I personally am always amazed at where my time went when my iPhone tells me my daily average every week. The truth is, with rare exception, we do have discretionary time. We do need time to unwind, connect with others, and meet our exercise and leisure needs. However, I am wondering if God might prompt you to make some changes in the way you spend your time to invest more in kingdom causes. Is there a ministry opportunity you simply need to commit the time to do?

I love that Jesus was a storyteller. Most of his great truths were taught to the people in parables, which were stories that used commonly understood items, jobs, and themes. I love his parable of the talents. I probably

7. Bureau of Labor Statistics, "American Time Use," 2.

love it for one of the wrong reasons, but truth be told, I love that the monetary valuation "talent" could easily mean "talent" in our current usage of the word.

Jesus tells the story of a man going on a journey. The man called together his servants to prepare them for his departure and his time away. He gave them varying amounts of his money, called talents, to take care of while he was away. To one he gave five talents, to another two, and finally he gave one to the remaining servant. Jesus makes a point of saying that these varying denominations of giving were also relative to the abilities of these servants. The man went on his journey and immediately the servant with five talents went to work trading in the marketplace and gained five more. The servant with two talents likewise invested or traded and made two more. The remaining servant took the one talent, dug a hole, and hid it in the ground. Eventually, the man came back and settled accounts with the three servants. The first servant proudly showed his master the five talents he had invested that turned into ten. The next servant showed the doubling from two to four talents as well. After each one, the master said, "Well done, good and faithful servant. You have been faithful with a little; I will set you over much." The final servant came forward and told him, "I know you are a hard man, reaping where you did not sow and gathering where you scattered no seed. So, I was afraid and went and hid your talent in the ground. Here, you have what is yours." I am sure he expected praise for protecting what had been given to him and returning it in its original condition. However, the master had a much different response. He angrily replied, "You wicked and slothful servant. You should have invested my money with bankers and I should have received my money with interest." He then took the talent and gave it to the one with ten, and cast the one-talent servant into the outer darkness.

As I said, the fact that the monetary amount is named a "talent" makes this easy to apply to how we use what God has given us. Sometimes in the past I felt bad for the servant who only got one talent. I wonder sometimes if some of us feel that we are a one-talent type of person. We might sometimes struggle to figure out exactly what the "gift" or "talent" is that God wants us to use. The truth is that a talent averaged about seventy-five pounds of gold. In February 2016, the average price of gold was approximately thirty-eight dollars a gram. This would put the average talent at $1.25 million in today's measures. The one talent dude was actually entrusted with a millionaire's share of responsibility. All three servants were given a huge amount of talent and responsibility.

We are not ordinary. We are "fearfully and wonderfully made." We have been endowed with millions in talents. The truth is also that nobody can replace *you* in the kingdom. God has a unique way he has wired and gifted you, and nobody else can replace or fill the role you were meant to play. To miss out on your purpose in using your talents is to miss out on God's special plan for you to impact the world in the most powerful way possible. The bigger issue is that if we miss the chance to use our talents for him, we miss getting to experience how he uses our little lives to do his big purposes.

From this parable, it is clear that Jesus is telling us to *invest* our talents and not bury them in the ground. He makes it clear that it is completely against God's will to sit on our abilities and, I would add, to misuse them. The first part of this investment is figuring out what these talents are. For some of us, we have known since we were a child what our unique abilities are. For some of us, we are still trying to figure it out. I love the acronym SHAPE from Rick Warren's *The Purpose Driven Life*:

S—Spiritual Gifts: What has God supernaturally gifted me to do?

H—Heart: What do I have passion for and love to do?

A—Abilities: What natural talents and skills do I have?

P—Personality: Where does my personality best suit me to serve?

E—Experiences: What spiritual experiences have I had? What painful experiences have I had? What educational experiences have I had? What ministry experiences have I had?[8]

"You will be most effective when you are using your spiritual gifts and abilities in the area of your heart's desire, and in a way that best expresses your personality and experiences."[9]

Many of you might be heart-deep in a ministry you love and know you are called to do. That is awesome. You are in your sweet spot of serving Jesus. I desire that for everyone, and so does God. If you are not, I encourage you to take a couple hours over the next week and pray, journal, and reflect on these five factors in understanding your mission. Warren has an online assessment you can use, or there are many others you can search for

8. Warren, *Purpose Driven Life*, 236.

9. Warren, *Purpose Driven Life*, 248.

on the internet. Your church might also have someone that can help you get started.

On that note, some of you might notice and even be offended that this book does not mention church much. Part of my mission is for you to understand your personal mission. I am not writing this as a pastor to get you to come to my church or follow me. I want you to understand God's Mission My Town for *you*. I certainly encourage you and would even expect you are pursuing some type of local church body, whether it be denominational, a local parish, or a home church. I want you to understand the mission within God's church. Much of this mission might be within the local church, and most of it will be outside of church buildings and in your town.

So, make an effort to understand your SHAPE. Ask God to lead you toward a ministry outlet to best utilize the unique, multi-million talented way that he has created you and developed you over your lifetime and experiences. And *do something about it*. Don't bury your talent in the sand. The misuse and disuse of your talents is not only sad to him, it angers him according to this parable. God desires us to join him in the amazing things he is doing around us. It is not about us doing great things for God as much as it is him doing great things *for* and *through* us. Let's set out on the adventure of using our treasure, time, and talent.

JOURNAL AND REFLECTION QUESTIONS:

1. S—Spiritual Gifts: What has God supernaturally gifted me to do?

2. H—Heart: What do I have passion for and love to do?

3. A—Abilities: What natural talents and skills do I have?

4. P—Personality: Where does my personality best suit me to serve?

5. E—Experiences: What spiritual experiences have I had? What painful experiences have I had? What educational experiences have I had? What ministry experiences have I had?

16

Beyond Hope

CIRCLE OF INTENTION: THOSE "BEYOND HOPE"

THIS PAST SUMMER, LORI and I were doing a camp assignment at a Young
Life camp property called Creekside, or more accurately, Washington
Family Ranch. It is in the middle of nowhere in Oregon. You drive on gravel
roads, then dirt roads, to get there and are often the only headlight on the
road for hours. However, you get there and it is spectacularly beautiful in
a very unique, desert-like way. As you get close, you drive through a tiny
town called Antelope that has thirty-five residents. As I drove through this
town for the first time, I was struck that such a simple, small, down-to-
earth town was part of a crazy story.

I couldn't help but picture in my head what it had been like for these
few residents between 1981 and 1985 when over three thousand cult members moved just down the road and took control of the town.[1] This story
reads like a science fiction novel.

Before Washington Family Ranch was a Young Life property, it be-
longed to Bhagwan Shree Rajneesh. He established a cult in Oregon after
being forced out of India. In India, he had established his ashram, which
became quite popular. People would travel for miles and miles to hear him
speak and to meditate with him in groups. Grateful, wealthy elite gave him
gifts and money. He became rich, but unpopular with the locals of Poona,

1. Moore, "Cult Site," line 11.

where his ashram was located. Many Westerners came and stayed and were reputed to finance their stays with drug running and prostitution. It is still unclear how directly these were related to the ashram. Due to the emphasis in the ashram on sex and the negative view that his followers had in the town, Bhagwan was called "the sex guru" by locals. Eventually, he was forced out of India.[2]

The Bhagwan then ended up buying thousands of acres in Central Oregon for $5.75 million.[3] By 1981, several thousand of his followers had gradually moved out to "Big Muddy Ranch" in very rural Wasco County. They even bought enough land and developed enough clout that the tiny rural town of Antelope was renamed Rajneeshpuram.[4]

Rajneeshpuram was a decidedly mystic place. "Active meditation" was emphasized. This was more like a grand mal seizure, where participants were encouraged to thrash about, scream, and moan, all in the hopes of getting the body so busy that the mind could be freed for enlightenment. In the "encounter group," acts of violence and sex were emphasized, with the line sometimes being blurred between the two. Teachings centered around the themes that free sex is fun, materialism is good, and Jesus was a madman. More specifically, the Bhagwan taught that prosperity was good, because God was in everything physical.[5]

The Bhagwan was partial to Rolls-Royces and began to buy about two per month. His collection gradually reached an upwards of ninety.[6] Each afternoon at 2:00 p.m., he would do his "drive-by blessings" as his followers lined the sides of the roads. They would shower his hood with flowers, then all head back to work. He also had a routine of getting in one of his Rolls, accompanied by security Jeeps with armed guards, and driving an hour to Madras, where he would get an ice cream soda. While he enjoyed this treat in his car, his followers would dance around his vehicle in loud fashion.[7] What the Bhagwan didn't fully realize is how difficult it would be to develop the available building and supporting utilities for a ranch zoned for farm use only. Eventually, he bought a building in Antelope and moved a bunch of his followers into this building. Several eventually ran for city council,

2. Wikipedia, "Rajneesh," line 18.
3. Aney, "Oasis in Desert," line 22.
4. Moore, "Cult Site," line 17.
5. Moore, "Cult Site," lines 20–22.
6. Aney, "Oasis in Desert," line 25.
7. Aney, "Oasis in Desert," line 25.

with four of them winning and taking a majority. They swiftly moved to rename the town Rajneeshpuram and worked to change zoning for the commune out on the ranch.[8]

This began a thirst for more power as they tried to influence and take over the greater Wasco County. They bussed in homeless people, offering free bus fare, food, and shelter. The population of the commune swelled to abouts seven thousand—a huge amount with only about twelve thousand total voters in the county. The Oregon government realized what was happening and stopped all voter registration in Wasco County, requiring each and every person to meet with a lawyer to decide whether their true intent was to live in the county. Bhagwan and his second-in-command, Ma Anand Sheela, or simply "Sheela," realized that these homeless people wouldn't be able to vote afterwards, and bussed them to Madras, Bend, or the Dalles, placing a real economic and societal burden on these communities.[9]

Desperate to still have a voice in the upcoming election, there was an attempt to reduce the total number of voters through an act of bioterrorism. Someone from the commune spritzed salad bars in the Dalles with cultured salmonella bacteria, causing over 750 people to get sick.[10] This obviously created a lot of animosity and negativity surrounding the Bhagwan and his followers, and his income and followers began to decline. Coupled with a growing contentious relationship with Sheela, things began to fall apart. Criminal charges soon began to mount and both Sheela and the Bhagwan fled the country, leaving behind a confused group of followers and a property very much changed over these few years.

Left behind were simple homes, greenhouses, shops, barns, a dam, a huge building where the worship took place, and even an underground maze of tunnels that the Bhagwan had built for security and a belief that there was an imminent nuclear attack. People even found two laboratories that had been set up to develop biological and chemical weapons. After the Bhagwan and his followers left, the property was like something you might see on "Lost" or some made-for-TV movie.[11]

But then something amazing happened. Montana billionaire Dennis Washington purchased the property for $3.65 million.[12] He hoped to

8. Zaitz, "Rajneeshee Leaders," lines 30–42.

9. Zaitz, "Rajneeshee Leaders," line 114.

10. Wikepedia, "1984 Rajneeshee," line 1.

11. John, "Rajneeshpuram," line 14–15.

12. Aney, "Oasis in Desert," line 32.

transform the property into a destination resort. But he also began to have zoning issues. Amazingly, Washington decided to donate this property to Young Life in 1996, in addition to giving a sizable financial donation as well.[13]

What was once a cult property is now the largest Young Life property that I have ever seen. The huge building where his followers once worshipped the Bhagwan is now a hub of activity for teenagers. Basketball courts, climbing walls, skateboard ramps, and much more. The remodeled Rajneeshpuram hotels are now dorms where hundreds of teens get to experience fun and depth in their nightly cabin times. The Bhagwan's nightclub and mall now house the Young Life staff and workers that make the place amazing as they serve kids. The property is now so large and developed that two Young Life camps happen every week on the property and the other three hundred campers don't even really know the other camp is there.

God redeemed this place. His hand is all over the redeeming of this cult property to one where hundreds of kids each summer make decisions to follow Jesus for the first time or step out in their faith anew. His redemptive details are all over this property. As the developers were deciding what to do with the Bhagwan's house, they sensed an eeriness and spiritual discomfort as they prayed over the house and what to do with it.[14] Entering the house seemed like a true spiritual battle. As they were trying to decide what to do, a finger of a wildfire raced down a hill and burned the house, the only one of over three hundred of the Rajneesh buildings to burn.[15] Property developers were trying to figure out how to have a manmade pond for water activities. However, it was found that it would evaporate ten thousand gallons per day.[16] The project went on hold as a pool was developed. As the pool was dug, the workers hit a natural spring, which had a flow of ten thousand gallons per day. There is a huge grassy field, where every week the kids enjoy games, skits, soccer, and sand volleyball. However, as the field was being developed, planners realized they would need several inches of sand to mitigate for muddiness. As this project stalled, a worker on a four-wheeler exploring the property found a sand deposit, which ended up providing almost exactly the amount needed for the field.[17]

13. Aney, "Oasis in Desert," line 34.
14. Moore, "Cult Site," line 65.
15. Aney, "Oasis in Desert," line 64.
16. Aney, "Oasis in Desert," line 61.
17. Aney, "Oasis in Desert," line 67.

You are probably wondering why so much detail about this camp. I myself am the type of guy who fought off sleepiness in every history class I ever took in school. I don't find myself gravitating toward historical happenings, but this Young Life property speaks to God's redemptive power. I personally am deeply touched, as I have seen hundreds of my high school friends experience Jesus' saving power and one of the greatest weeks of their lives at this property. As I look at the story behind the Bhagwan and this property, the faces of my high school friends come to mind. What the Bhagwan intended for anything but Jesus Christ has become a place in the world where some of the most effective heart change for teenagers happens every week of every summer.

This property, at one time, seemed "beyond hope."

My friend in the Body Shop seemed "beyond hope" as well. I was an assistant basketball coach and graduate student at Eastern Washington University while working at the Body Shop. This was a circuit-based fitness center on the campus of EWU. My role was to set up programs for students and others who used the facility, as well as help them with proper technique and training practices. The Body Shop was designed around a rotation of fitness machines on a timed schedule. This job involved a tremendous amount of conversation for me.

"Jake" was a regular at the Body Shop. Although fairly interested in fitness, he was utilizing the Body Shop as a physical education credit opportunity and sometimes seemed less than motivated. Jake was a life-of-the-party type of guy. He was fun to talk to and wanted to engage in conversation pretty much every time he was in for a "workout." During Jake's visits, I talked to him for probably a collective twenty-five hours over the course of the year, very little of it (if any) having to do with muscle contractions, breathing techniques, or posture.

Jake was fun to talk to; rather, fun to listen to. Conversations were often one-sided and Jake loved telling his stories. Sometimes I would cringe inside on Mondays when Jake walked into the Body Shop. I knew that Mondays were most often going to be about the parties he attended over the weekend, the crazy antics he saw and participated in, how many shots he drank, what type of joint he smoked, and often which girl he slept with (which often wasn't his girlfriend at the time). These conversations were really awkward for me, and Jake just couldn't read the discomfort in my eyes. Jesus had grabbed my heart by this time, but my wisdom was still a step behind. Rather than telling Jake about my discomfort, I would listen quietly, never really engaging, but not frequently re-directing the conversation. After months of these types of conversations, I finally found the courage to tell Jake my discomfort.

I tried to explain why these conversations were so awkward and hard for me. I explained that I was a follower of Jesus and that many of his life experiences were completely different than what I was trying to live out. He asked a few questions. I gave answers that I am sure were more about law than they were about love. I tried to explain how I was waiting for marriage in terms of sex. I tried to explain that I didn't believe in drinking to get drunk. I tried to explain that I valued how I treated other people. In short, I talked about actions and beliefs, but I am not sure I effectively conveyed that it all had to do with how much I loved Jesus and wanted to honor him and bring him glory. My lack of courage contributed to this conversation happening with about a month left in the school year. The remaining few weeks were very awkward when Jake came to the Body Shop.

I think, when I have looked back at this time and scenario in my life, that I lacked courage. I also believe I lacked wisdom for the right words to say. But since then, what God has taught me in looking back is that I lacked faith. I really thought Jake was "beyond hope." His lifestyle, decisions, and morality seemed beyond anything that Jesus could touch. When I really think about it, I believe "the conversation" I finally had with Jake was more about me being uncomfortable than it was about influencing Jake toward Jesus. I am not sure if you work with or deal with anyone like Jake. They might be so profane, so unloving, so corrupt, so full of vice, so full of deceit, that if you were honest, you would deem them "beyond hope."

Jake brought about another situation that I have only personally had happen to me once so far in my life. And I don't want to ever have it happen again.

After the summer, I was in my second year at the Body Shop. Jake needed more PE credits. So, come September, in walks Jake. My heart sank a bit, honestly. Before logging in and beginning his workout, he asked if we could talk. My job being flexible and not busy at the time, I was able to have my co-worker cover for me. Jake took me in the hall and proceeded to teach me more about God and myself than I ever knew. Jake was the prototypical cocky, entitled, privileged, and selfish person that one finds easy to resent. He always looked at you with a mix of conceit and "guess what I just did" attitude. But this day was completely different.

Jake put his hand on my shoulder and looked me in the eye. This was different. A hint of a tear appeared and a look of utter humility. I immediately had goosebumps all over. Jake simply asked me, "Why didn't you tell me?" Silence filled the space. More silence ensued. I had no idea what he was talking about it and he suddenly realized it. "Why didn't you tell me about Jesus? Why didn't you tell me about your faith?" He knew I was a Christian, but didn't hear from me what it actually meant. He had only seen difference in me in the way I interacted with him and others, but I hadn't communicated *why* once I had the chance. The next period of time was life-changing for me. My faith in God was bolstered as Jake, whom I had considered "beyond hope," told me about the circumstances that summer in which Jesus had grabbed his heart, and he had decided to follow him. Jake told me his story with humility, wonder, and joy about how God had shown him how much he loved him, and that Jake had been trying to find his own meaning in empty things. Jake told me how much he respected me, had seen something different in me, and had been waiting for me to share what this difference, this faith, really meant to me. I had missed out.

But once again, even relationships are not "beyond hope."

During that conversation in the hall outside of the Body Shop, God showed me this in a powerful way. Jake said he wished I would have told him, but now he wanted to ask me something. My heart was in my throat by this time, but I said, "Sure, anything." He proceeded to ask me if we could meet periodically to talk about spiritual things. He still had the same girlfriend and they both had come to faith. They were taking steps backward to honor God physically and wanted accountability. He wanted me to support him as he came back to the same place and to many of the same people and situations, but as a radically different person himself. He wanted support in learning to live like Jesus desired. I loved my God even deeper that day. I saw a God that could redeem even our mistakes of omission.

The next year with Jake was amazing. I got to walk with Jake as he succeeded and sometimes failed in his mission to love and live like Jesus. What had been empty, sin-filled conversations between us were now filled with depth and truth. Jake had asked me to help in his faith development, but these conversations might have impacted me as much or more than him. My God taught me that nobody, no situation, no circumstance is beyond his power or reach.

In our Circles of Intention, God wants us to remember Paul.

Think about someone who has been unkind to you regarding your faith in Jesus. Recollect when someone made fun of you, belittled you, or showed you disdain for believing in an "invisible" God. Think about someone who made you feel small or unintelligent for professing faith.

Paul was much beyond that.

Paul was a severe persecutor of the church. He actually had Christians beaten, imprisoned, and killed. Paul hunted down people who professed faith in Jesus Christ and had them tortured. It would be hard to even think of a modern equivalent of the evil person that Paul is described to be in the Bible. You couldn't be much more "beyond hope" than Paul. Christians feared him for their lives. He hunted them down out of hatred. We might not have a better illustration of someone beyond hope.

But God caught his attention on a road and Paul's life was never the same. The Christian church was never the same either. This man who persecuted Christians became one of their most outspoken leaders. He wrote much of the New Testament and has brought hope and faith to millions of us through the Holy Spirit-filled letters he wrote.

We are wise to think about Paul and then think about who might be similar in our life. We would be wise to not think that these people are beyond the reach of our God. God has redeemed the lives of many people in history who seemed "beyond hope."

JOURNAL AND REFLECTION QUESTIONS:

1. Who is someone that comes to your mind when you hear the words, "beyond hope"?

2. Have you seen yourself, or anyone you know, radically transformed by Jesus? How so?

3. If you can think of someone "beyond hope" in your life, what will you do differently as a result to include them in your Mission My Town?

4. Find some of your favorite passages written by Paul in the New Testament. Reflect upon how this Jesus-hater became someone who has given us great direction and comfort for a couple thousand years.

17

Turn the Other Cheek

CIRCLE OF INTENTION: YOUR ENEMIES

I HAVE BEEN READING a book recently that has been rocking my world. Nik Ripken's *The Insanity of God* is a powerful book that I would recommend to all. He has traveled the world listening to and documenting the stories of believers in every corner of the world, most of whom suffer persecution that we will never understand here in the Western world. He tells story after story of how God actually uses persecution to draw people closer to him. In one story, he tells of a faith-based organization in an Islamic country.[1]

This Christian organization provided medical care to a people who were very much opposed to the message of Jesus, but very much in favor of the life-saving and health-giving care that this organization provided. Most of the Muslims were peaceful toward the workers at this clinic due to the care they received. However, some radical Muslims were very harsh and outspoken toward the clinic due to the beliefs of its people. Specifically, the most outspoken and militant critic lived right across the street from the clinic.[2]

The clinic was located near a mosque. On the days where many people were headed to the mosque, the man would stir up the passing crowds, inciting hateful and untrue charges against the clinic and its workers. He

1. Ripken, *Insanity of God*, 293.
2. Ripken, *Insanity of God*, 293.

would try to bring hate and mistreatment upon the people of the clinic. His anger and hatred was always on the brink of physical violence, but thankfully never took that form.[3]

This man eventually developed a fatal form of cancer. The shop that the man owned became shunned by the Muslim community, as they thought it contagious. The man was dying, but now also completely broke as his business failed. The clinic's workers heard of his plight and all began to purchase items at his shop to provide income. They asked about his health, his family, his life. Eventually, as his condition worsened, they began to treat him and washed his body on occasion.[4]

This man's heart of stone eventually softened as these people in the clinic cared for him tangibly. He became their friend. He even made the decision to follow Jesus near the end of his life. The amazing part of the story is that it continued from here. His young wife was now caring for four young children. She had seen the love and compassion that these believers had shown her husband and also became a follower of Jesus. This young woman became possibly the most effective witness in this area toward her Muslim friends and neighbors.[5]

All because people chose to actually listen to Jesus and apply his words.

"But I tell you, love your enemies and pray for those that persecute you" (Matt 5:44).

I love the Bible. I really do. But there are a few things that Jesus asks us to do, that I just say, *"Are you kidding me?"* I am still growing in my understanding of the ways and power of Jesus, so when I hear the following story, I can't even begin to fathom the truth of it.

Most of us have heard of Dylann Roof by now. The twenty-one-year-old white supremacist entered Emanuel African Methodist Episcopal Church during a prayer service on June 17, 2015. He proceeded to shoot and kill nine African Americans, including the senior pastor. I cannot even imagine that kind of hate. When confessing to the murder, he said that he hoped the shooting would ignite a race war.

One victim was a forty-five-year-old mother of three, a reverend, and high school track coach. Another victim was the forty-one-year-old Reverend Clementa Pinckney, who was also a state senator. A third victim was a fifty-four-year-old librarian. A twenty-six-year-old was killed who had just

3. Ripken, *Insanity of God*, 293.

4. Ripken, *Insanity of God*, 294.

5. Ripken, *Insanity of God*, 296.

graduated from college and was looking to begin his career. A fifty-nine-year-old wife of the reverend was also senselessly shot down. A seventy-year-old grandmother was also gunned down. A seventy-four-year-old grandfather and part of the ministry staff was also a victim. A forty-nine-year-old mother of four was also tragically gone forever. An eighty-seven-year-old woman was also brutally taken down.[6]

Mothers. Fathers. Sisters. Brothers. Sons. Daughters. Grandfathers. Grandmothers. Aunts. Uncles. Friends. Gunned down for the color of their skin while they served others by praying for the church.

As I write this, I catch a tear out of the corner of my eye while my thirteen-year-old daughter plays Minecraft on the computer, sitting on the couch with Annie, our four-year-old Shih Tzu. I hear my son's loud voice simultaneously wafting in through the open windows on this warm summer night. As I write, I hear my amazing wife laughing as she talks to a dear friend on the phone. As a side note, I realize that this isn't probably the best atmosphere for writing. But as I read about the victims above, they were all loved by someone like I love my family. In a senseless act, their abbreviated lives would now forever leave an empty hole in the lives of the people they loved. There is no way for me to comprehend the pain that such an event would hold.

And there is no way for me to comprehend the response of many of these loved ones.

During a bond hearing for Roof, the victims' families were given the opportunity to file in front of Roof and say a few words. Person after person came forward to talk about how they forgave Dylann Roof and were praying for him and his soul. As each person stood up and, many times through tears, forgave Roof, he didn't even bother looking up at any of them. They forgave a senseless hate crime done to people they loved dearly.[7]

Sometimes I have a hard time forgiving someone cutting me off in the Starbucks line. Sometimes I have a difficult time forgiving someone at work that I felt slighted me or didn't recognize the efforts I had made on their behalf. The list could go on. But to forgive like these people? I don't know that I have it in me.

But Jesus challenged us to a response that is not our own and not one that we can muster on our own power. Jesus certainly modeled it for us. Imagine for a minute being him. One of his best friends, who he spent the

6. Simeone, "These are Victims," paragraph 1–17.

7. Dickerson, "Charleston Victims," line 12.

last couple of years investing in, betrayed him. In a week's time, the crowds went from putting palm branches down in front of him and honoring him to later wanting him killed. He was mocked, whipped, beat, spit on, and made to carry a heavy cross on top of his tattered, bloodied body. Amazingly, Jesus prayed, "Father, forgive them, for they do not know what they are doing" (Luke 23:34). Jesus gave us the ultimate example of forgiving our enemies.

Remember when we took the time to draw out our Circles of Intention earlier in this book? My bet is that if you look back, you didn't include "enemies." I know I didn't. Enemies don't naturally come to mind when we think about people we want to impact. But I challenge you now to actually think about who your "enemies" are. My wife is a sweet person who does ministry full-time. Her enemies are few and far between. I have a very public job where if we don't win enough games, play someone's son, or run the right offense, people can choose to be my enemy. Living in a community, word usually circles around and I find out I had some enemies I never realized. Take the time to think about who in your own world takes offense or issue with you. You might even have people you take offense toward or just have issue with. They might be people you know through work, in your public or even private life.

I believe that Jesus wants us to work to positively impact even our enemies. Even more, I believe that when we do so, we impact people we never even expected to impact. And it is often unknowingly.

I think back to the two examples I mentioned earlier in the chapter: the Muslim man and Dylann Roof. I have never met the people in these situations who chose to forgive their enemies, but I am certainly impacted. Just as in the case of Dylann Roof, our enemies may show no noticeable signs of responding to or acknowledging our forgiveness and active love. But frequently, it speaks volumes about Jesus to others who are watching and observing our lives. It might only be your family, kids, or close friends. It might be a whole country of people. But the way we deal with our enemies will either be like the culture, or it will be like Jesus. The way of Jesus is so starkly different than the entitlement of the world that people will be put on notice.

I don't believe it is a good life and social strategy to try to collect enemies so as to witness to them. But whenever people are gathered and work together, live together, minister together, or do life together, there will be friction and problems. The apostle Paul certainly had his enemies. As we talked about in the last chapter, he lived most of his life persecuting Christians, thereby gaining enemies. He then was sold out to Jesus and was persecuted by the Jewish religious leaders, and gained enemies on that side of the fence too. But Paul tells us in Romans 12:18: "If it is possible, as far as it depends on you, live at peace with everyone."

Let's be a people who are known for working for peaceful relationships with others. And when that is impossible and people choose to be our enemies, let's have the response of Jesus. If we want to be salt and light and truly be different and impact those around us, this response will go a long way in doing so.

JOURNAL AND REFLECTION QUESTIONS:

1. Who is someone that would be considered an enemy to you? Reflect upon why this is so.

2. When is a time you chose to forgive someone who wronged you? Do you still feel that same forgiveness in your heart now for this person?

3. I spoke of a couple crazy forgiveness stories. What are others that you have heard about or experienced?

4. Do you need to ask for someone's forgiveness for being an enemy toward them? What steps will you take?

18

Earn the Right to be Heard

THE AWKWARD MOMENT SEEMED to last an eternity. My well-meaning, passionate, but socially challenged college friend—we will call him "Jon"—intently looked across the college cafeteria table at my other friend, whom we will call "Tyson." Jon leaned forward with an earnest look in his eyes, waiting for a response from Tyson. Tyson's eyes darted from Jon's to mine with a look that could kill, or at least thaw an Alaskan glacier. The obvious irritation and annoyance was clearly visible for everyone at the table. Except Jon. He still waited eagerly for an answer to his question to Tyson. This evening was the first time my two friends had met. In fact, they had met less than two minutes prior to this moment of icy awkwardness. We sat down for a meal at the college cafeteria when Jon found us and joined us.

I loved Jon and had spent time with him through Bible studies and we were both growing in our faith and excited about Jesus. Tyson, my roommate, Bruce, and I were close immediately at the start of school that year. The very first weekend in our dorm brought us together. During a dorm initiation night, we found ourselves the only ones not downing Solo Cups of alcohol. Bruce was an on-fire Christian who that year radically and completely changed my view of what it meant to follow Jesus. He vowed to be a difference-maker for Jesus and had chosen that his non-use of alcohol would be a way to witness to others. Tyson came from an alcoholic family and had seen family members succumb to a pattern that led them and their families to great pain and loss. He had chosen not to drink accordingly. I, on the other hand, was coming out of a time of my life where I would have easily joined in with what was happening. But, because I was drawn to Tyson and Bruce and was hanging out with them, I chose to hang with them and not participate in what else was going on.

Tyson, Bruce, and I became close and spent much time together. As Bruce's roommate, I was watching someone who lived for Jesus 24/7. I saw someone that had *faith* and not simply *belief,* such as I had. I saw someone who had made Jesus *Lord* and not simply *God.* I saw someone who had a *relationship* with Jesus. Meanwhile, Tyson and I were on the basketball team together. He was the handsome, precocious, ultra-athletic guy who the girls immediately liked and guys wanted to be around. He was twice the player I was without putting in a fraction of the time. He was fun, funny, and people loved being around this confident, even cocky, but funny guy. And he was a very self-proclaimed atheist. We were an interesting trio. Bruce: sold out and following Jesus. Me: trying to make sense of the rote experience I had made my faith, but yearning for more. Tyson: an atheist who spent almost every waking hour with us who were Christians. This brings me back to the original story. Tyson now icily looked at Jon. The annoyed, piercingly blue eyes of Tyson met the earnest brown eyes of Jon. I said a quick prayer. I am sure Bruce did the same. Before I could think of a way to diffuse the situation, Tyson shoved his food across at Jon, got up abruptly, and walked out of the cafeteria.

Jon, within two minutes of knowing Tyson, had abruptly asked him: "Are you a Christian?" There was no lead into this question. There was no context for this question. There was no relationship to ask this question. Jon just asked it out of the blue, in hopes it would initiate a spiritual dialogue of some type. He had no idea of the hours that Tyson, Bruce, and I had already spent peacefully talking about beliefs, God, and eternity. He had no idea about Tyson's annoyance with well-meaning Christians who pushed their view on him.

I often wonder how people's approach to impacting others for Jesus has done more harm than good.

I don't mean to offend anyone or limit the power of God. I know God works in ways that are so far beyond what I understand. I know he uses many means to allow people to get to know him.

But I also wonder: how many of you have found Jesus by reading a booklet handed to you by somebody on the street? How many of you have started a relationship with Jesus by having someone hold up a sign outside of a concert saying that you are going to hell? How many of you started a relationship with Christ by reading a sign at a rally or a protest? How many of you know Jesus today because a stranger stopped you on the sidewalk to tell you about Jesus?

It is very possible that some of you have one of these experiences as your story.

However, how many of you have a faith and relationship with Jesus that was inspired by a mentor, friend, or relative who gave you an example of what it means to follow Jesus?

My guess is that more of you have this story.

Many people come to faith through a public speaker or a conference or other means. However, the biggest impact for most people that I have met, is having people in their life that love them, care for them, and speak to them through their everyday life. Then, when appropriate, they use words. Most people I know have been impacted by *relational* ministry.

We have spent our time together looking at the different Circles of Intention on which you can focus your Mission My Town. I firmly believe that Jesus wants us to use these circles to build relationships, and *earn the right to be heard*. Through building relationships, we create the trust to talk to people about our Jesus.

I think of Jon and Tyson's exchange. Jon did Tyson more harm than good. There was an absence of relationship, timing, and the Holy Spirit's leading. I compare that to the hours of conversation that Tyson, Bruce, and I had over pizza boxes on our dorm floors—over conversations Tyson and I had during van rides to games. Tyson knew we loved him regardless of what he believed about Jesus. He knew and saw the difference that Jesus was making in every corner of our lives. He didn't come to a relationship with Jesus at that time, but he was exposed to it daily.

Lori and I discovered very early in working with high school kids that they didn't care much at all what you had to say until you showed you cared for them. Trying to impact anyone in a positive direction, whether it is spiritual or any type of personal development, starts with earning "cred." Credibility comes from relationship first, then showing you have some knowledge or expertise to impart. Lori and I had some great student leaders who wanted to impact the people around them. In an effort to help them, we needed to be more intentional and give them some tools. In conjunction with things we had learned, read, and experienced, we developed some steps to "earn the right to be heard." We first encouraged these student leaders to start with the end in mind. The goal is to develop relationships that turn into friendships and provide opportunity to have maximum impact. To have maximum impact, we need to "give out of our overflow," "enter the other's world," and then "be ready." In trying to develop faith in others, the very first requirement is to have something to give. As mentioned previously, you can't give what you don't have. In working with our student leaders, we came alongside them to help them come to a place in which spiritual disciplines were part of their daily life. Praying, journaling, reading the Word, spending time in worship and fellowship are a huge part of being close to God. The first concept is to "give out of the overflow." Our own faith needs to first be sincere and real. In order to have spiritual "cred," others need to see a winsome faith in us first that is attractive and authentic.

Secondly, we encouraged them to "enter their world." The best way to impact people and develop relationships with them is to spend time with them in natural ways. This might involve playing sports or video games together. It probably would include showing interest in things that interest them, such as attending their games, going to their concerts, or simply giving genuine attention to their interests. One thing that all of us have in common is that we eat. Have people over for BBQ, go get bubble tea, meet at Starbucks, or go get pizza. Someone once told me that his strategy is "BBQ first." That is to say, in developing friendships, as well as impacting others for Jesus, he found it best to do natural things first, like having a BBQ.

Jesus showed this principle on many occasions. He met people at wells. He dined with "sinners and tax collectors." He initiated conversations with people on the road. Paul gives us great insight as well: "I have become all things to all men so that by all possible means I might save some. I do all this for the sake of the gospel, that I may share in its blessings" (1 Cor 9:22–23). Paul did the work of learning about the local people, understanding their culture, and building relationships, so as to impact them for Jesus.

The last step with which we challenged these student leaders was to "be ready." We have finally "earned the right to be heard," and our friend is now sitting across the dinner table, leaning in to hear about this Jesus we have been living for and praying to; we have a chance to clearly communicate our faith. I am a firm believer in being spiritually ready for these significant conversations. Let's explore this now in the next chapter.

JOURNAL AND REFLECTION QUESTIONS:

1. Do you feel like you ever ministered to someone in an ineffective manner because you weren't really listening to the Holy Spirit, but rather to your own understanding?

2. How are you doing with each of the following elements of your impacting others: giving out of our overflow, entering their world, being ready to communicate God's love?

3. What current relationships do you have with non-believers in which you are "earning the right to be heard"?

4. Who is someone you can think of with whom the next logical step in your relationship and your influence would be to make more time to "enter their world"?

19

Significant Conversations

BOLDNESS TO SPEAK

The majority of my life has been spent with high school students. I have taught for twenty-five years, and I have done ministry through Fellowship of Christian Athletes and Young Life for most of these years. I love high school kids and enjoy the process of trying to help them navigate these tricky years, which are fraught with a unique mixture of hope and disappointment. Their altruism is met with the reality of the world they experience. They are often hopeful and hopeless all at the same time. The high school kids I love and work with every day have a far more difficult world to navigate than I did as a high schooler. The quickness, ease, and type of images and information that high school kids access every day is staggering.

Their lives are changing quickly and constantly. Even as adults we have seen technology change the way we do business, life, and relationships in many ways. Our lives are changing quickly as well and this can be best shown through social media.

Some of you might have even used Myspace. Don't take offense if you are still using it, but the social media evolution has long left Myspace in the dust. Facebook has become a dominant social media for most of the world. More than one billion people across our great planet log in to Facebook daily. As a side note, my high school friends look at Facebook as something they use to communicate PG-13 content and pictures with grandparents and other adults whom they see as ancient. You might also use LinkedIn to put your best professional foot forward in an internet-based world. Many of us have wasted more than our fair share of time on YouTube. My high school friends spend hours on YouTube. Most of us use it to look up how to tile a bathroom or change the headlights in our 2002 Jeep Grand Cherokee. Many people also use Pinterest or even Tumblr. The truth is that social media popularity will change by the time you read this book.

When looking at social media, a few observations stick out as parallels to society and culture. Facebook was the original big beast. People love posting pictures, videos, albums, motivational messages, and so on. Some people will even tell you where they eat every meal, complete with a visual. Many Facebook posts are fairly long. Then came Instagram. As an "Insta" user myself, how cool is it to post a quick picture and a short message? In my world, with my followers and vice versa, these are usually a sentence or two. Or maybe even a sentence fragment. Twitter has been around for a while also. It has been made either famous or infamous for its use by our current commander in chief. In 140 characters or less you can try to tear somebody down, communicate, motivate, or just rant. Snapchat seems to be the dominant social media with students right now. Users send a quick message that will be live from anywhere between one and ten seconds, at which point it self-destructs. We live in a world dominated by social media. We have access to quicker and more information than any generation in history. We communicate quickly and often with friends, family, and followers. I enjoy the ability to keep track of family and friends all over the world.

But do we think more deeply than any generation in the history of the world?

Do we communicate with others in a meaningful manner?

Are we losing some of our ability to connect deeply with other people?

So, in a world so connected, why would the *Huffington Post* say that we are currently living in the "age of loneliness"?[1] It is estimated that one in five Americans live in persistent loneliness.[2] That seems crazy given that we can communicate more easily with others compared to any time in the history of the world. There are conflicting results about the role that social media plays in this dynamic. As Facebook is the dominant social media

---

1. Gregoire, "Why Loneliness," lines 1.
2. Gregoire, "Why Loneliness," lines 1–2.

site, much research has been done on the effects of its users. Below is an excerpt from the New Yorker on this topic:

> The key to understanding why reputable studies are so starkly divided on the question of what Facebook does to our emotional state may be in simply looking at what people actually do when they're on Facebook . . . When people engaged in direct interaction with others—that is, posting on walls, messaging, or "liking" something—their feelings of bonding and general social capital increased, while their sense of loneliness decreased. But when participants simply consumed a lot of content passively, Facebook had the opposite effect, lowering their feelings of connection and increasing their sense of loneliness.[3]

In other words, the world of constant connectivity and media, as embodied by Facebook, is the social network's worst enemy: in every study that distinguished the two types of Facebook experiences—active versus passive—people spent, on average, far more time passively scrolling through news feeds than they did actively engaging with content. Demands on our attention lead us to use Facebook more passively than actively, and passive experiences, no matter the medium, translate to feelings of disconnection and boredom.

A person who does a lot of college ministry told me recently that college students start going "crazy" after just a few minutes in a room without their phones or a computer. "One would think we could spend the time mentally entertaining ourselves," he said. "But we can't. We've forgotten how. Whenever we have downtime, the Internet is an enticing, quick solution that immediately fills the gap. We get bored, look at Facebook or Twitter, and become more bored. Getting rid of Facebook wouldn't change the fact that our attention is, more and more frequently, forgetting the path to proper, fulfilling engagement. And in that sense, Facebook isn't the problem. It's the symptom."[4]

I can see these truths in myself. Attention has forever been altered. I also wonder if our lack of depth and real conversation has impacted our relationships and ability to share our faith. You can only share so much in 140 characters. I wonder, in our Twitter-dominated society, how much of abundant life we miss out on by *not* engaging in meaningful conversation

---

3. Konnikova, "How Facebook," paragraph 7.
4. Konnikova, "How Facebook," paragraph 11.

and dialogue. It is also another reminder that we are created in the image of the God. Part of this image is a need to connect. With God. With others.

Last year, I attended a funeral for a former player's father. Owen had courageously battled brain cancer for far longer than the doctors had ever imagined was possible. As I drove to the funeral, I reflected on how these events typically go. People say amazing things about the character, life, and impact of the deceased. It is often amazing to see the degree of impact people have had on others. I thought about how powerful it would be for the deceased to see and hear this impact. The truth is, funerals are more for the living than the deceased in many ways. They never get to hear many of the things that are spoken about them at their own funerals.

What I encountered at this service really affected me. This service was full of life and humor. Owen had been given a gift in that he knew he was to die soon. His son, Jordan, was able to take video of Owen in his last few weeks, telling stories and giving final thoughts. The whole family knew Owen was going to heaven, had seen him suffer, and was happy to see this suffering end and heaven begin. One thing that impacted me greatly was the number of people present. Owen's coworkers showed up in droves. People from the community in which we live poured into the church. People that Owen had partnered with on mission trips to the Dominican Republic showed up. Jesus was made known. He was made known through the video of Owen sharing. He was made known by the joy and love with which Owen's kids and siblings spoke of him. And many people from all walks of life heard about why Owen was how he was. He had been a deep follower of Jesus.

As I drove home that afternoon, I was so amazed at Owen, and his life. I also made a vow to myself that day. Nobody that was close to me would not know, *truly know*, how I felt about them and what I appreciated about them and the legacy that they had. I didn't want to say a single thing at a friend or family's funeral service that I hadn't already clearly let them know.

I began a list. Prayerfully, I began to think and list people. I wanted to have fifty significant conversations with people God led me to talk to, before the end of the next year. I devoted a journal to listing these people in my life and then recording the nature, theme, and feelings after each of these conversations. I very creatively titled this pursuit my "50 Significant Conversations."

This has been a life-giving, affirming adventure. I am thirty-one conversations into my fifty and it has been at least as encouraging and faith-building for me as it probably has been for those with whom I have met. I start each meeting with these significant people in my life by preparing in prayer. I spend time beforehand, coming before Jesus and asking what he would have me say to each of these people. I think about my history with each person, their future, and what God might have for them. My list is a mix of dear friends, family who knows me better than anyone, unbelieving friends with whom I have never really shared Jesus, young people who I want to encourage towards leadership and service to Jesus, mentors who have left deep imprints on my life, my wife, and my kids.

So far, I have also done something that most of you would find strange. You see, I want these significant conversations to not only encourage these people by letting them know how they have enriched my life and what gifts and abilities that I see in them, but I want more. I want these meetings to not only inspire, but also make Jesus known. So, whether I am meeting at a Starbucks over a venti iced coffee, on a lake deck over a beer, or at a restaurant over scrambled eggs and bacon, I imagine an extra chair. This "chair" is a reminder for me to pray my way through these times. I want to include the Holy Spirit in what could be the most important conversation I have with some of these people. I recently met with a former friend that I have discipled and haven't seen in a few years. I knew I wanted to catch up, let him know the mark he left on my life, but then it got fuzzy. Going into the conversation, I really didn't know what else God wanted me to communicate. So I prayed. I listened.

Over breakfast food, I suddenly felt like God had something that he wanted me to communicate. Out of nowhere I said, "God wants you to be the cycle-breaker." I knew without a doubt that the Holy Spirit wanted me to speak these words, although I didn't know why until I saw a tear in the corner of my friend's eye. God suddenly gave me words to connect the story of my friend's deep family drama and dysfunction growing up to how God wanted him to break the cycle and give his wife and kids a different legacy. We had an awesome conversation and my faith grew as I re-learned that God often has things he wants us to share with others if we will just pray and listen.

I wonder who God wants you to have a real conversation with. I wonder if there is somebody who knows you well, with whom you have earned the "right to be heard," but haven't had the courage to approach them about anything related to your faith.

One of my recent significant conversations was like that. It was with one of my colleagues and friends I see every day at work and often in social situations. Our kids are friends and we share a circle of friends. We have spent a lot of time together on a boat, at work, eating out with a group of guys, joking, and laughing. Scott knows I love Jesus. He knows I serve different ministries. He sometimes jokes about me going to synagogue or Bible club. I would usually smile, shake my head and move the conversation on to something else. We have had many real conversations about parenting, coaching, teaching, and life. But I was not bold in getting past the surface about Jesus.

Scott is a dynamic person and has a wide network of friends. He is affable, an extreme extrovert who people follow easily and enjoy being around. His students love and appreciate him and adults enjoy being around him due to his sense of humor and fun personality. I wanted to encourage him in these things and let him know what a powerful effect he has on so many young people and colleagues alike. I also knew it was time to get past the surface and talk about Jesus. I am not a huge beer guy. However, in the right time and place, I will have a beer. This was one of those places and times. Scott was almost giddy when I showed up on his porch and told him to go pour us a beer. For the nex thirty minutes I shared the amazing gifts of personality and influence that I saw in him. I shared the power he had to impact people for good. And I finally talked about Jesus. For the first time, he was open about where he was in his journey in his faith. His dad had died a couple years ago, his brother had experienced some huge pain in his life as well, and Scott was looking at the meaning behind all of these things. It was a great time of opening the door to spiritual conversation; hopefully Scott knows that proverbial door is always open.

If you listen, I mean *really listen* to the Holy Spirit, he will guide you in ways that you never would consider. One of my most recent significant conversations happened while vacationing on Kauai with some very close friends. Jeff has been a close friend for fifteen years, and I was really looking forward to recognizing his amazing ability to be a consistent, intentional, and faithful friend. Additionally, he really is a Barnabas-like figure in the lives of those of us who call him "friend." Barnabas was known as the son of encouragement and Jeff fits this bill. I was also excited to encourage Jeff for the tremendous steps in leadership he had taken in his new job and challenge him toward thinking about what was next. But the Holy Spirit wanted me to talk to him about something else.

I didn't want to do it. I honestly gave the Holy Spirit an inner eye roll and said, "Whatever." I sensed he really wanted me to challenge Jeff on a particular relationship. I knew this was a very sensitive and non-peaceful relationship for Jeff. I just didn't want to be the one to bring it up in this conversation, but the Holy Spirit honestly told me inside: "I want you to do this for Jeff's sake." So, I shared that I felt like God really wanted Jeff to consider this relationship and if there was any way of him looking at it differently.

Jeff looked at me and his eyes narrowed. The proverbial shat was about to hit the shan. Instead, he asked incredulously, "Have you been reading my journal?" Jeff then proceeded to tell me that three days earlier he had woken up early in the morning wrestling in his spirit and couldn't sleep. He climbed out of bed, hopped on a trail, and soon found himself alone on a beach in the pre-sunrise hours. He told me that as he sat on the sand watching the ocean and the sunrise, God spoke to him more clearly than he had in some time. "Fresh starts." As Jeff thought about this, God gave him the mission for this year to look for "fresh starts" in his relationships and dealing with people. And clearly, the relationship I pressed him on was a huge part of this theme. Jeff and I continued to talk through it and had an amazing time together. I felt privileged to hear from God, pass it on to Jeff, and realize that I was just part of the way God was communicating to Jeff on this issue. How humbling and amazing to see God at work through us just getting out of the way and being open to him.

I am really looking forward to more of my 50 Significant Conversations and seeing what else God does. I love it so much and it has had such an impact on myself and others that I just want everyone to experience the power of getting beyond the surface and going deep. I want everyone to get past the fear of rejection, awkwardness, or possibly offending someone and have a true conversation about where people are in their faith journey.

I have been blessed to have the following experience a couple of times: someone I have known for a long time asks me, "What is it that makes you different?" Once I realize that they are not talking about being sometimes awkward or having a corny sense of humor, I feel that by "different" they mean something positive. On these occasions, somehow they have seen Jesus working through me and want to know more about it. These are the moments for which I live. However, the truth is, these experiences don't happen as often as I would like. You probably are more spiritually mature than I am and have this happen daily. If so, I need to read your book. I feel extremely blessed to say that I have the opportunity to have many spiritual conversations. I don't attribute this to any great measure or myself. Rather, a few years ago, I began praying specifically for opportunities throughout the day to have depth in conversation and to have conversations that lead to talking about spiritual things. More specifically, I have found that praying for these opportunities for specific people in my life almost has always led to chances to do so.

Throughout our time together we have talked about our Circles of Intention. We have looked at being intentional in our approach to impacting people in these circles. Now, I challenge you to pray for and seize the opportunity once it presents itself.

Who needs *you* to be bold and approach them? *Who* is *ready* to hear about your faith? *Who* is *God* asking *you* to spend time with and have real communication? I am excited for you to ask these questions, hear the answer, and *do* something about it.

JOURNAL AND REFLECTION QUESTIONS:

1. Who needs you to be bold and approach them?

2. Who is ready to hear about your faith?

3. Who is God asking you to spend time with and have real communication?

4. What was the last spiritual conversation and how did it go? Who comes to mind when you pray for your next conversation?

20

Mountaintop Experiences

It is a moment I hope I will always remember. My daughter sat on the edge of a hotel bed with a look that was a mixture of appreciation, joy, thankfulness, contentment, and peace. McKaden stroked the long woven yellow and black scarf around her neck as she spoke, her eyes traveling its length with joy. As a huge Harry Potter fan, the Hufflepuff scarf was at that moment the representation of the past couple days we had just shared. This scarf spurred her comment as she spoke her next words, which resonated in my heart, and hopefully always in the memory banks of my Dad mind.

"I will always cherish this."

While she probably specifically meant the scarf at the time, I really do believe it was the overflow of her heart and experience that we had just shared together. McKaden and I were about to wrap up her "13-year-old" trip when this moment occurred in a hotel in Burbank, California.

My wife and I have a goal to really *live* and *give*. We are not so much into things. Our life is not about acquiring fancy, expensive cars or houses. We want to be rich in experiences and relationships. So, Lori gave me the freedom to do something that has been very meaningful to me, and hopefully my kids. We have done a 10-year-old trip and now a 13-year-old trip. We sit down together and plan the trip based on a budget and their interests and passions.

When she was ten, McKaden wanted to be a paleontologist. She came up with the idea to travel to see fossils and dinosaur artifacts. Together, we planned out a three-day trip to Western Montana. It was an amazing road trip where we went to three different dinosaur museums and even went out to an actual dig site with a real paleontological team. We ended up at the Museum of the Rockies in Bozeman, which boasts one of the greatest exhibits in the country. We had two nights in hotels, many miles and hours winding through beautiful Montana roads, lots of ice cream and fast food, and amazing memories.

For the 13-year-old trip, we went a bit bigger. I actually surprised her three days before we were to leave and told her we were going to go to Universal Studios. Lori and I had already purchased the tickets and made hotel reservations. The main draw was the new Harry Potter portion of the park. We even purchased special passes to get in an hour earlier to this part of the park. McKaden then helped me plan the remaining time there, which consisted of spending a whole day at the California Natural History Museum across from USC. It was a three-day experience of things she absolutely loved.

We built memories together through these shared experiences. Max's trips looked totally different as his passions and interests vary dramatically from my daughter's. For his teen trip, I surprised him by us flying into San Francisco and meeting up with my good friend and his son, who is one of Max's good buddies. For three days, we did an "Amazing Race" experience where we opened envelopes for the boys to figure out how to get to our next adventure. It was three days of fun, laughter, friendship, and male bonding. The specifics of *what and where* are not the big point here. The point is the *why*. I was able to have some very significant conversations with my kids that were carefully timed to where they were in those stages of their lives. We not only built memories, we built relationship. It is time and even money that I will never, ever regret spending.

These mountaintop experiences helped create circumstances that hopefully impacted my kids and created margin to have great conversation that was accompanied by laughter, joy, and experience.

These are all the same things that make great impact for your Circles of Intention. I realize that what I was describing up to now was about my kids. I have shared other mountaintop experiences with my Circles of Intention that led to significant conversations and deep spiritual impact. These were intentional, planned events and circumstances that culminated in time, space, and atmosphere, in which real conversations could be had and heard. These are experiences that captivate the heart of those we love and create a culture of fun, care, depth, and intentionality, and provide opportunity to let them know how much we truly care about them. This, in turn, hopefully leads to a glimpse or even a conversation about how much Jesus cares about them.

Jesus was the master of mountaintop experiences. His disciples had this type of experience with him multiple times. Not only did they get to be part of his inner circle and experience everyday life with Jesus, they often got to experience situations in which Jesus intentionally took them to be part of something that made them grow. I think about how cool it must have been for Peter, James, and John. In Mark 9, Mark describes how Jesus specially chose these three and "led them up a high mountain." I think about the speculation these three ordinary guys must have had as they trudged higher and higher up a mountain, not knowing where Jesus was taking them. By this time, with all the crazy wonders they had seen from Jesus, the anticipation must have been building with every footstep. And Jesus did not disappoint. He was transfigured so that his clothes became "dazzling white." Words can't even describe seeing their friend and leader shown once again to be clearly God. Imagine the wonder, surprise, and even fear as they then saw Moses and Elijah. These men who Jesus called close friends, and who he knew would be leaders in the church, got to catch a glimpse of God.

I challenge you to find ways to create or participate in mountaintop experiences so that those you desire to mentor and lead can catch a better glimpse of Jesus as well. Maybe it's time you rented the houseboat and took your buddies on the trip of a lifetime. Maybe it is time you and your inner circle of friends went to a women's conference that you had been talking about attending. Maybe it's time you leverage your connections to ask for the use of that fishing cabin to take your close friends for a long weekend. Jump in the plane, car, boat, ferry, or train with your kid. Create an experience through which they know you love them. Create an experience that is so special they can't help but see that you value them. Create an experience that provides margin to have real fun, real conversation, and real connection between you and your Circle of Intention.

You won't regret it. Life is short; get out of the ordinary.

JOURNAL AND REFLECTION QUESTIONS:

1. Who is someone that comes to your mind that you would love to take on a mountaintop experience?

2. Who has provided this type of experience for you?

3. Reflect on some experiences you have had over your lifetime. Reflect on the power and the outcome you experienced.

4. Spend time journaling some dream experiences within your budget that might be fun to someday provide for those you love.

21

Making Disciples

"Therefore go and *make disciples* of all nations"—Matt 28:19 (emphasis added).

IN OUR JOURNEY TOGETHER, we have explored:

–Where God has us right now in our lives and what he is calling us to do.

–Having a vision and Mission My Town.

–Being in a place in our faith where we can be salt and light to our town.

–Being prayerful and wise about impacting our Circles of Intention.

We are closing our time with our biggest call to the people in our Circles of Intention. Jesus, in some of his last words to his followers, told them, "Go and *make disciples*," and I would add, "of my town." We want to be sure that we not only have a mission, and clearly identify those to whom we want to mission, but that we don't miss the whole point of what we are missioning them *toward*.

A quick Google search will tell you that a disciple is "a follower or student of a teacher, leader, or philosopher." Webster tell us that synonyms are "follower or adherent." Our greatest mission, and hopefully desire, is to see those people in our Circles of Intention become followers or students of Jesus. Not just believe in him, but truly become students of Jesus, his life, his words, his mission, and his ways. We want to point them toward Jesus and then help them learn about how to go past that and become a *disciple*.

I would suggest that if we aren't actively making disciples, then we are passively missing the point of how Jesus asked us to impact the world.

We have looked at our Circles of Intention. Now we are going beyond that to look at who you are in a unique position to disciple. Who is looking to you for leadership and direction in their own faith? This is a question that deserves an answer. It might be your grandkids. It could be the little brother that you spend time with through big brothers. Possibly it is a group of your college suitemates that are looking at how you are living for Jesus. It might be an organized Bible study through a church or through a campus ministry. Either way, we need to find the people God wants us to actively and intentionally *disciple*.

Let's not get scared off by the responsibility of this task. Let's not over-spiritualize it either. Let's look at how Jesus discipled (obviously) his *disciples*.

Jesus did basic life with these people. He ate with them, drank with them, wept with them, and traveled with them. I think about my college friends, Bruce, Matt, and Mike, who discipled me. I am not sure we had many formal Bible studies, but I got to go with them as we ran errands, had lunch, and just had time to hang out and talk. They discipled me in these moments through their actions and active faith. They were never afraid of talking about Jesus at any moment. Do you have someone that you are hoping to disciple? Take them with you on car rides, invite them to breakfast, go to the spa together, just do life together, and be prayerful about opportunities for spiritual conversations in the midst of this.

Another way Jesus discipled his dozen was to take intentional teaching times. He told parables to the masses and it is often said that he later spent time explaining them to his disciples. Honestly, the most dynamic disciple-maker I have seen lives under my very roof. Lori has an extremely high capacity and heart for discipling other women around her. She is also a gifted teacher and speaker and uses these gifts both publicly and in smaller settings. At any given time, she has two or three different groups of women who are going through different books or parts of the Bible. Her groups consist of names like Oasis, Village, and Anchor. The amazing thing to me is seeing how much time and excellence she invests in each and every one of these groups. She not only reads the books, but she backs up her preparation with deep Bible study.

Your discipleship might take this form as well, and you have more resources than ever to lead such groups. Go on Amazon and search for books that would hit your needs head-on. Find a podcast series that you can listen to together. Go old-school and do a Chip Ingram or Beth Moore study that has books, DVDs, and a workbook. The material is important, but the culture is equally so.

People grow when they are supported, yet challenged. Provide an atmosphere for your disciples where there is full-on grace. I believe that transformation is impossible without transparency. Transparency can't exist where judgment, or fear of being judged, exists. At the same time, we want ourselves and our disciples to become more and more like Jesus. I encourage you to keep people accountable to reading, studying, and attending, all the while loving them unconditionally.

Jesus also allowed his disciples to experience some peak experiences with him and some special times away from the crowds. As referenced earlier, he brought Peter, James, and John with him to undergo three miraculous experiences. While we might not raise the dead together, we can experience more of God with our disciples. Take your "Peter, James, or John" with you when you get to speak. Let them hear you teach or preach for Jesus if that is something you get to do. Plan and execute a getaway with your disciples. Rent a beach house. Rent a fishing cabin. Get out the backpacks and climb a mountain. Borrow a house at a cool location. Find a unique and special way to not only spend time together, but have intentional thought and preparation for some spiritual moments on these special times away. I have found some of my most powerful times experiencing God and closeness to others on these types of adventures.

One important part of making disciples is making sure you are a disciple. As we already learned: you can't give what you don't have. Get close to Jesus and your impact on your disciples can't help but be more influential. In an effort to be a disciple, I would encourage you to be in a mentor relationship also. In our efforts to mentor and impact others, we also can always go deeper with God. There is no way we can ever fully know an omnipotent and omniscient God.

Allow a mentor to speak into your life. Find someone who has traveled the path that you desire to travel as a parent, professional, or believer. I have found that mentors can best speak into our lives when we have some common life missions. Carefully find this person and give them license to ask the tough questions, to have access past the front porch of your life, and to be transparent in a way that helps bring about transformation.

JOURNAL AND REFLECTION QUESTIONS:

1. Do you currently have a mentor in your life? Describe this relationship. If not, reflect on who might be able to fit this role in your life.

2. Are you currently discipling a person or a group? Reflect on how this is going and how God might take it even deeper.

3. If you don't have a group or person you are discipling, reflect and pray about who God might be leading you towards.

22

What Now?!

TIME TO GET TO WORK

IT'S TIME FOR OUR journey together to come to a close. However, I hope and pray that this time has challenged you to a new heart and attitude about where Jesus has you right now in your life. Equally important, I hope that this time has called you to action. As James, the brother of Jesus, said: "Dear friends, do you think you'll get anywhere in this if you learn all the right words, but never do anything?" (Jas 2:14). I have read books that have inspired me to an emotional high. I have read books that have educated me and changed my point of view. I have read books that have really made me think about my life and place in God's plan. But the most influential books are the ones that have brought about a change in my *heart* and *actions*. This is what I pray for you.

Own this place and time in which God has placed you.

Really. *Own it*. Not some mission trip you took ten years ago. Not some camp high you experienced and long for from time to time. Not the future, when everything in your life is lined up just right to go into missions or serve him more effectively. Not after you get out of college. Not looking back before you retired and had more energy. Not once your finances are better. Not once you know more about the Bible. Not once you get rid of all your bad habits. Not comparing it to the ministry experience you had a decade ago. Own *now*. Discover and own the purpose that Jesus has for you in the present. After all, no other time truly matters.

If you are like me, you long for the life that Jesus desires. I often confuse *his* life for me for *my* life for me. I want to understand clearly what his life and plan look like for me and then experience it. The truth is that we can have it. Jesus had a very clear message for us on this.

I think of Jesus as portrayed in John 10. I visualize him looking out over a crowd with a look of love and a prayer to his father to give him the right words. Quiet settles over a crowd as the simply dressed, bearded man begins to speak. I picture an audience divided. There were Pharisees and other Jews in the audience with brows wrinkled in a mix of anger and fear. These were people that were looking to catch Jesus saying something that would condemn him. There were also eager, earnest faces peering at Jesus as he began to speak. These people had seen the emptiness of a faith and life built on ritual sacrifices, trying to earn righteousness by observing law after law, many of which made little sense in their connection to actual God and faith. By contrast, I see a bold, confident Jesus as he begins to explain his life mission and purpose. Jesus minced no words, but he used words that would resonate by using concepts with which these people were familiar.

Jesus patiently gave example after example. He used word picture after word picture. He spoke about entering the sheep pen through the gate. He spoke about shepherds. He spoke of himself as the true gate. He spoke of himself as the good shepherd. And in the middle of this, he gave us words that stop me in my tracks as I read them and visualize the scene.

"The thief comes only to steal and kill and destroy. I came that you may have life and have it abundantly" (John 10:10).

Wow. In a short verse, Jesus tells us so much. He relays that Satan and the world unaffected by God wants to steal and kill and destroy. There are countless aspects of our lives that the enemy wants to steal, kill, and destroy.

Joy.

Hope.

Love.

Goodness.

Faith.

Our personal purity.

Our witness to others.

Our purpose in life and living.

Peace in our hearts, minds, and relationships.

The spread of the gospel and God's purposes above all else.

Just take a minute to think about how the world and Satan are robbing you of all these things above. Think about what things in culture, social media, and so on work to rob and reduce all of these things in your life.

Jesus wants to give us all these same things. The express purpose that Jesus came was to give us a life full of these things. Not necessarily full of big houses, boats, jewelry, big bank accounts, or social media fame. Jesus came to give us life that is abundant in all his spiritual treasures. I love that Jesus desires for us not just to experience a life in him and his blessings, but a life that is *abundant*. This is one of my favorite verses in the Bible, as it shows how much Jesus loves us and how much he desires for us to experience so much beyond what we are oftentimes experiencing. *Abundant life.* How often do we live in fear, lack of purpose, anxiety, and confusion? I challenge you to think about what life abundant would look like for you *right now, where you are.*

Jesus wants us to walk far from Satan and what he would steal, kill, and destroy in our lives. He wants us to walk with joy and purpose in the freedom that he has given from these things. I believe that abundant life is best found in doing what God has called you to do, right where you are.

I have found through my own experience that we typically remember a very small amount of what we read. Even from a great book, I typically remember a couple important lines and two or three themes. Some books don't leave a mark in my memory at all. Some books I need to read and read again so as to soak up the message that I feel I need to learn. Our experience together can best be summed up by the title, of course: *Mission My Town.* We are on a mission right where we are. Otherwise, we run the risk of missing the purpose of being where God has placed us. I will finish with a quote that I believe really gets at the heart of what God wanted me to share through this time with you. Everything about this quote summarizes what we have been processing through together.

"You go where you're sent and you stay where you're put and you give what you've got."—Jill Briscoe[1]

1. https://www.facebook.com/jenniesallen/photos/go-where-youre-sent-stay-where-youre-put-and-you-give-what-youve-got-till-youre-/15747155589220327/.

I pray that you are obedient and *go* where God sends you without excuse.

I pray that you would listen and stay when God asks you to stay.

I pray that you would discover your gifts and your unique self that you can offer others.

And lastly, I pray that you would give everything you have to this special place that God has you in right now.

Abundant life. Let's experience nothing less than what God wants so he can use us to impact the people around us.

Thanks for journeying with me.

Epilogue

Journeying Together

WHEN I WAS IN my early twenties, I discovered the wonder of backpacking and hiking. God gave me an appreciation for wandering trails and discovering his brilliance around me. Through a college outdoor recreation class, I experienced snowshoeing trips and multiday backpacking adventures in the great Pacific Northwest (PNW). We did group trips and I made new friends that I otherwise never would have had. I also learned things about God and his creation that I would never have seen.

Shortly after my senior year in college, I experienced what I thought was a difficult breakup with a girlfriend. My response to this was to bravely and stupidly head off on a week-long adventure in the wild, by myself. It was awesome and awful at the same time. A couple nights I found myself feeling fear in the middle of the night as I heard the sounds of the deep forest. I ran out of some supplies that limited my comfort greatly. But on the positive side, I once found myself quietly sitting beside a mountaintop lake, overlooking a valley that stretched for miles below me, with not a hint of another human being. I experienced breathtaking views juxtaposed with moments of deep loneliness.

I feel that the writing of this book had elements of both of these experiences. I am not naturally self-disclosing and I found myself in the "wilderness" of sharing things with you that I might not, were we to be face-to-face. I found myself often in the loneliness of writing and struggling to hear from God. But I also found great partnership among those who came alongside me to help me in this venture with proofing and providing critical insight. I experienced some fellow travelers in the writing of this book. I thank Ryan and Lori for honest feedback. I thank my editor Ashley, who patiently provided much needed feedback and direction. I thank Lori, Max, and McKaden for being patient as there were many nights that kept me behind my computer keyboard. I thank my parents and siblings who have supported me and modeled so many of these "Mission My Town" concepts in their own lives. My parents and siblings are private people and therefore not mentioned here. However they are very much weaved into so many parts of my story and what I have learned to pass on to others. I have mentioned my small group brothers already, but I also want to recognize a couple friends who also have influenced me greatly. My friends Matt and Rick have shared life and faith with me for many years. We have had real and raw conversations about health, family, parenting, work, and faith. We lift each other up, sharpen each other, and provide honest feedback in love. All these people have been fellow travelers on this book journey.

I am now asking you to be a fellow traveler as well at the completion of these pages.

I wrote this book because it is the book and words that God placed in me. I wrote it due to my life of working through the same questions that you all likely have. I wrote it because I want to see Jesus magnified. I want to journey together as you apply these concepts in your own life.

It would be a great gift to me to hear your stories and how God takes your intentionality and begins to use it in the Circles of Intention around you. It would be a great gift to see how he uses these words to impact his kingdom through a fellow brother or sister and spiritual traveler. So, please feel free to contact me and share your victories and your experiences. I have shared many of mine and would be honored to hear yours. I love hearing how people join God in what he is doing around them. Allow me to be a support and encouragement to your journey.

Your fellow traveler,

Mark
missionmytown@gmail.com

Bibliography

Aney, Kathy. "Oasis in the High Desert." *Local* (blog), *East Oregonian,* July 17, 2015, https:// www.eastoregonian.com/news/local/oasis-in-the-high-desert/article_23c0923a-8ca5-5c5f-b622-03e97ba8a7fd.html.

Batterson, Mark. *All In.* Grand Rapids: Zondervan, 2013.

Barna Group. "Research on How God Transforms Lives Reveals a 10-Stop Journey." *Faith & Christianity* (blog), *Barna,* March 17, 2011, https://www.barna.com/research/ research-on-how-god-transforms-lives-reveals-a-10-stop-journey/.

Bureau of Labor Statistics. "American Time Use Survey—2017 Results." U. S. Department of Labor, June 28, 2018, https://www.bls.gov/news.release/pdf/atus.pdf.

Chanatry, David. "America's 'Most Polluted' Lake Finally Comes Clean." *National* (blog), *NPR,* July 31, 2012, https://www.npr.org/2012/07/31/157413747/americas-most-polluted-lake-finally-comes-clean.

Dickerson, John S. "Charleston Victims Wield Power of Forgiveness." *Opinion* (blog), *USA Today,* June 22, 2015, https://www.usatoday.com/story/opinion/2015/06/21/ charleston-church-shooting-families-forgiveness-column/29069731/.

Forrest, Adam. "I'll Have Jesus, with a Little Idolatry on the Side." *June 2012* (blog), *Zondervan Blog,* June 5, 2012, https://zondervan.typepad.com/zondervan/2012/06/ ill-have-jesus-with-idolatry-on-side-excerpt-idleman.html.

Gregoire, Carolyn. "Why Loneliness is a Growing Public Health Concern—And What We Can Do About It." *Science* (blog), *Huffington Post,* March 21, 2015, https://www. huffingtonpost.com/2015/03/21/science-loneliness_n_6864066.html.

Idleman, Kyle. *Not a Fan.* Grand Rapids: Zondervan, 2011.

Ingram, Chip. *Living on the Edge.* New York: Howard, 2009.

John, Finn J.D. "Rajneeshpuram: Did it Almost Turn into an Oregon Jonestown?" *2010* (blog), *Offbeat Oregon History,* May 30, 2010, http://www.offbeatoregon.com/ H1005e_Bhagwan4of4.html.

Konnikova, Maria. "How Facebook Makes Us Unhappy." *Annals of Technology* (blog), *The New Yorker,* September 10, 2013, https://www.newyorker.com/tech/elements/how-facebook-makes-us-unhappy.

LCRA. "Highland Lakes and Dams." *Water* (blog), *LCRA,* 2019, https://www.lcra.org/ water/dams-and-lakes/Pages/default.aspx.

Mishler, Randy. "Rajneeshees: From India to Oregon (Part 1 of 20)." *Rajneesh* (blog), *The Oregonian,* February 19, 2019, https://www.oregonlive.com/rajneesh/1985/06/ rajneeshees_from_india_to_oreg.html.

Moore, Art. "Oregon: From Cult Site to Teen Camp." *1999* (blog), *Christianity Today,* November 15, 1999, http://www.christianitytoday.com/ct/1999/november15/9td022. html.

Nance-Nash, Sheryl. "Is the Bible the Ultimate Financial Guide?" *Leadership* (blog), *Forbes,* May 24, 2012, https://www.forbes.com/sites/sherylnancenash/2012/05/24/ is-the-bible-the-ultimate-financial-guide/#1a4f6dc36493.

Ripken, Nik. *The Insanity of God.* Nashville: B&H Publishers, 2013.

Saviuc, Luminita D. "Why the Greatest Gift You Can Give Someone is Your Time." *Love & Relationships* (blog), *Purpose Fairy,* November 30, 2018, https://www.purposefairy. com/68394/why-the-greatest-gift-you-can-give-someone-is-your-time/.

Simeone, Jessica, et al. "These are the Victims of the Charleston Church Shooting." *Jessica Simeone* (blog), *BuzzFeed News,* June 19, 2015, https://www.buzzfeed.com/ jessicasimeone/these-are-the-victims-of-the-charleston-church-shooting?utm_ term=.duQo54XvX#.bad5awNDN.

Snohomish County. "Lake Stevens Details." https://www.snohomishcountywa.gov/5393/ Stevens.

Stearns, Richard. *The Hole in our Gospel.* Nashville: Thomas Nelson, 2010.

———. *The Hole in our Gospel Book Summary.* Givers by Design. https://www. giversbydesign.org/wp-content/uploads/2013/04/Book-Summary-The-Hole-in-Our-Gospel.pdf.

Warren, Rick. *Purpose Driven Life.* Grand Rapids: Zondervan, 2002.

Wikipedia. "1984 Rajneeshee Bioterror Attack." *Article* (blog), *Wikipedia, The Free Encyclopedia,* accessed May 2, 2019, https://en.wikipedia.org/w/index. php?title=1984_Rajneeshee_bioterror_attack&oldid=891835501.

———. "Dylann Roof." *Article* (blog), *Wikipedia, The Free Encyclopedia,* accessed May 2, 2019, https://en.wikipedia.org/w/index.php?title=Dylann_Roof&oldid=895025433.

———. "Lake Karachay." *Article* (blog), *Wikipedia, The Free Encyclopedia,* accessed May 2, 2019, https://en.wikipedia.org/w/index.php?title=Lake_ Karachay&oldid=892666814.

———. "Rajneesh." *Article* (blog), *Wikipedia, The Free Encyclopedia,* accessed May 2, 2019, https://en.wikipedia.org/w/index.php?title=Rajneesh&oldid=895037106 .

———. "Ronald Wayne." *Article* (blog), *Wikipedia, The Free Encyclopedia,* accessed May 2, 2019, https://en.wikipedia.org/w/index.php?title=Ronald_ Wayne&oldid=894093058.

———. "Steve Jobs." *Article* (blog), *Wikipedia, The Free Encyclopedia,* accessed May 2, 2019, https://en.wikipedia.org/w/index.php?title=Steve_Jobs&oldid=893820901.

———. "Steve Wozniak." *Article* (blog), *Wikipedia, The Free Encyclopedia,* accessed May 2, 2019, https://en.wikipedia.org/w/index.php?title=Steve_ Wozniak&oldid=894690437.

Zaitz, Les. "25 Years After Rajneeshee Commune Collapsed, Truth Spills Out — Part 1 of 5." *Rajneesh* (blog), *The Oregonian,* April 14, 2011, http://www.oregonlive.com/ rajneesh/index.ssf/2011/04/part_one_it_was_worse_than_we.html.

———. "Rajneeshee Leaders Take Revenge on the Dalles with Poison." *Rajneesh* (blog), *The Oregonian,* April 14, 2011, https://www.oregonlive.com/rajneesh/2011/04/part_ three_mystery_sickness_su.html.